Cambridge Elements ≡

Elements in the Philosophy of Religion
edited by
Yujin Nagasawa
University of Birmingham

GOD, SOUL AND THE MEANING OF LIFE

Thaddeus Metz
University of Johannesburg

CAMBRIDGE
UNIVERSITY PRESS

CAMBRIDGE
UNIVERSITY PRESS

University Printing House, Cambridge CB2 8BS, United Kingdom

One Liberty Plaza, 20th Floor, New York, NY 10006, USA

477 Williamstown Road, Port Melbourne, VIC 3207, Australia

314–321, 3rd Floor, Plot 3, Splendor Forum, Jasola District Centre, New Delhi – 110025, India

79 Anson Road, #06–04/06, Singapore 079906

Cambridge University Press is part of the University of Cambridge.

It furthers the University's mission by disseminating knowledge in the pursuit of education, learning, and research at the highest international levels of excellence.

www.cambridge.org
Information on this title: www.cambridge.org/9781108457453
DOI: 10.1017/9781108558136

First published 2019

A catalogue record for this publication is available from the British Library.

ISBN 978-1-108-45745-3 Paperback
ISSN 2399-5165 (online)
ISSN 2515-9763 (print)

God, Soul and the Meaning of Life

Elements in the Philosophy of Religion

DOI: 10.1017/9781108558136
First published online: April 2019

Thaddeus Metz
University of Johannesburg

Author for correspondence: Thaddeus Metz, tmetz@uj.ac.za

Abstract: This Element critically explores the potential relevance of God or a soul for life's meaning as discussed in recent Anglo-American philosophical literature. There have been four broad views: God or a soul is necessary for meaning in our lives; neither is necessary for it; one or both would greatly enhance the meaning in our lives; one or both would substantially detract from it. This Element familiarizes readers with all four positions, paying particular attention to the latter two, and also presents prima facie objections to them, points out gaps in research agendas and suggests argumentative strategies that merit development.

Keywords: meaning of life, God, soul, immortality, justice

ISBNs: 9781108457453 (PB), 9781108558136 (OC)
ISSNs: 2399-5165 (online), 2515-9763 (print)

Contents

1 Introducing the Philosophy of Life's Meaning

What, if anything, makes our lives meaningful? How would a spiritual dimension, such as a Heaven transcending the realm of nature, bear on life's meaning? Is God or a soul essential for a meaningful life, or at least for a particularly meaningful one? Or might these spiritual conditions in fact seriously detract from the meaning available to a life?

This Element seeks to acquaint readers with contemporary philosophical answers to these questions. Its primary aim is to recount key authors, texts, claims and arguments from the recent literature composed by analytic philosophers. A secondary aim is to advance enquiry by, amongst other things, pointing out weaknesses in positions that need to be addressed and suggesting under-explored strategies that merit consideration.

The overarching theme of the Element is that there has been a shift in much of the debate about the extent to which, and respects in which, spiritual conditions such as God or a soul bear on the meaning of our lives. During the medieval and modern periods in the West, the debates were principally about whether God or a soul is *necessary* for any meaning in our lives.[1] Supernaturalists then usually claimed, or at least implied, that something spiritual is indeed required for meaning in our lives to be possible, such that, if we live in a purely physical world, then all our lives are meaningless. Naturalists, in contrast, denied that claim, and instead maintained that meaning is *possible* in the absence of God or a soul. These days, many supernaturalists no longer claim that meaning as such is impossible without God or a soul, instead tending to maintain that a *great* meaning would be impossible without one or both of them. Not only have naturalists denied this claim, but some have also gone on the offensive by arguing that the presence of God or a soul would in fact *reduce* our odds of obtaining meaning in certain ways.

This Element addresses both the classic positions, which may be described as 'binary' for being all or nothing when it comes to meaning's logical dependence on a spiritual dimension, as well as the newer developments in the field that focus on degrees or ranked kinds of meaning available to human beings. It pays particular attention to the latter views – advanced largely over the past dozen years – that God or a soul uniquely would either greatly enhance the meaning in

---

[1] The use of the specific word 'meaning' and the cognate term 'significance' is a pretty recent, modern phenomenon, substantially appearing in the past 250 years or so (Landau 1997). However, the reader will recall that more than 2,000 years ago, the author of the Biblical book Ecclesiastes proclaimed that 'all is futility' and that life is akin 'to the pursuit of wind' (discussed later in this Element). And when Thomas Aquinas, for instance, enquires into the final end for human beings, he is thinking about what the point of our lives is or what our highest purpose is, which is more or less about life's meaning. Although the words are different, the concepts are at least similar.

our lives or detract from it (and conceivably both, in different respects). The Element aims to contribute to philosophical reflection on these matters (although not to defend specific conclusions about them), and to enable other philosophers, theologians and related thinkers to do so.

This Element's enquiry into religious matters addresses the way that the presence or absence of certain spiritual conditions might bear on life's meaning, and not the way that a certain belief system or social practice might do so. So, the philosophical disagreements addressed here are not so much about whether, say, having faith in God or being part of a congregation confers meaning regardless of whether God exists, but instead about how the truth of theism, viz., the reality of God, might confer it (perhaps upon His existence being acknowledged by a believer) or not.

With regard to how spiritual conditions might affect life's meaning, this Element considers only philosophical literature, and does not appeal to, for instance, testimony from purported prophets or holy texts, works in religious studies or findings from empirical psychology. In addition, the philosophical texts it takes up are solely those from the Western, and then the particularly English-speaking and analytic, tradition. Relatedly, this means that the Element addresses the potential influence on life's meaning of God or a soul as they are characteristically conceived in the Abrahamic faiths, leaving aside spiritual conditions salient in other worldviews, such as ancestors in traditional African religion or Brahman in Hinduism.

The next Section of the Element defines central terms, specifying what is meant by words such as 'God' and 'soul', discussing the meaning of 'life's meaning' and distinguishing the sense of 'supernaturalism' from views such as theism (Section 2). In particular, it draws a key distinction between the meaning in a person's life and the meaning of the human race as a whole, with much (though not all) of the Element addressing the former topic, regarding a final value that may be exhibited in some individual lives but not others, at least not to the same degree. The Element then explores the 'extreme supernaturalist' view that God or a soul is necessary for human life to be at all meaningful, sketching the central rationales for the view and their prima facie weaknesses (Section 3). In the following Section, the Element critically discusses the view that neither God nor a soul is necessary for a meaningful life and that a purely physical world would be sufficient for some degree of meaning (Section 4), explaining why this 'moderate naturalist' perspective has become so common to hold in the post-war era. After that, the Element considers the claim that, while a spiritual realm is not necessary for a meaningful life, only it could significantly enhance the quantity, quality or duration of meaning available to us (Section 5). Upon having considered what there is to be said for this 'moderate supernaturalism', the Element takes up 'extreme naturalism', according to which we would instead be better off in terms of meaning if there were no spiritual realm (Section 6). According to this perspective, God or a soul would detract from the meaning available to us. The Element concludes by noting that it is too early to expect firm views about these matters, given how recent are the non-binary positions that spiritual conditions would add to, or conversely subtract from, life's meaning in substantial ways. The conclusion also sketches promising ways for readers to make contributions to these cutting-edge debates about God, soul and the meaning of life (Section 7).

2 Clarifying the Terms of the Debates

The aim of this Section is merely to define the words central to the debates explored in the Element. We need clarity about what counts as, say, 'supernaturalist' or 'meaningful' in order to ensure that interlocutors are not speaking past each other and to be confident of what a certain position involves. The Section begins by analyzing what talk of 'life's meaning' means for a large majority of analytic philosophers (2.1), then defines terms central to competing theories of what would make life meaningful (2.2) and finally considers how metaphysical matters, about the nature of reality, are conceptually distinct from theories of meaning, but nonetheless might substantively affect their plausibility (2.3).

2.1 The Concept of Life's Meaning

The dominant view amongst twenty-first-century English-speaking philosophers about the concept of life's meaning, that is, what competing theories of meaning are all about, is that it is a variable final value that is usefully distinguished from other final values such as happiness and morality. There are some sceptics about that, who contend that talk of 'life's meaning' is superfluous and could be replaced without loss by appeal to another condition good for its own sake, particularly talk of 'well-being' (e.g. Kershnar 2014; Hammerton 2018). Rather than use space to argue against such a deflationary view of what meaning-talk is about,[2] this Section articulates the view widely accepted by those party to debates about the role spiritual considerations play in life's meaning, viz., that meaning is not reducible to any other single final value.

For most these days, talk of 'life's meaning' (and of synonyms such as 'significant existence' or 'important way of being') signifies a cluster of conditions that are good for their own sake and that can come in degrees. In particular,

---

[2] Say, by showing how meaning can intuitively come from sacrificing one's own net well-being for the sake of a cause.

life is usually taken to be meaningful by definition to the extent that it makes sense, forms a narrative, merits 'fitting' reactions such as esteem or admiration, manifests value higher than animal pleasures, realizes a purpose or contributes positively to something beyond itself. Few believe that any single one of these properties exhausts the concept of meaningfulness, although some do (e.g. Nozick 1981: 574–612; Martela 2017). Instead, for most in the field, when we think or speak about life's meaning, we have in mind at least one of these features and quite often more than one as an amalgam (Markus 2003; Thomson 2003: 8–13; Mawson 2016; Seachris 2019).

Notice that the aforementioned features of the concept of meaningfulness are at least analytically distinct from happiness, construed subjectively, and moral praiseworthiness, construed impartially. That is, when we have meaning in mind as a quality human life can exhibit, we are not thereby conceptually considering merely whether a person's life is pleasant or satisfying to her, or whether she has given others their rightful due. Substantively, it might be that one's life is in fact (more) meaningful insofar as one has been happy, and perhaps even happy in the course of doing morally right by others. However, the present point is that this is not true by definition of the phrase 'life's meaning'. Some meaning could, conceptually speaking, come from conditions that are non-happy and non-moral, perhaps a scientist slaving away to make a discovery about the nature of the universe. Indeed, it is not a contradiction in terms to wonder whether meaning would come from a life that is unhappy and immoral, say, that of a tortured artist who has ditched his wife and children to make great paintings that he will not show to the public.

So far, the meaning of 'meaning' has been expounded, but there is also unclarity about what the word 'life' might signify. A large majority of contemporary philosophers have focused on the meaningfulness of the lives of human persons, with them having undertaken little enquiry into whether lives of animals can exhibit meaning or even whether the lives of human non-persons, such as the extremely mentally incapacitated, can do so (but see Purves and Delon 2018).[3]

When it comes to the lives of human persons, there is a common distinction drawn in the field between the meaning 'of' life in general and the meaning 'in' a particular life. The former is roughly about whether there is a point to the existence of the human race as a species, or, more carefully, human persons as a natural kind. Is there a purpose for which we were all created, or is there a way for humanity to connect with something highly valuable beyond itself, or how

---

[3] There have been some, however, interested in the meaning of the universe or finite reality as a whole, not merely of the human race to be found in it. Here, there is often posed the question of why there is something rather than nothing (e.g. Edwards 1972; Mulgan 2015; Tartaglia 2015).

might one be able to tell a good story about the human race? One readily sees why God, especially, has been so frequently invoked to answer these kinds of questions.

The latter issue, regarding the meaning in a life, is about whether and how a given person's life can be meaningful. What, if anything, about one of our lives can merit considerable pride or admiration, or which goods should a person seek out that are worth much more than base pleasures, or how, if at all, can one live in a way that would ground a compelling autobiography?

Standard answers to these questions in the Western tradition appeal to the famous triad of 'the good, the true and the beautiful'. The 'good' in the first instance signifies beneficent ways of relating, e.g., advancing justice, giving to charity and loving family and friends. The 'true' refers to intellectual enquiry and ideally understanding, ranging from a formal education about the natural world, on the one hand, to wise self-awareness, on the other. The 'beautiful' picks out creativity, and so initially brings to mind composing or interpreting artworks, but it could also consist of, say, being funny or devising a novel technological gadget.

Both religious and non-religious theorists commonly deem these to be characteristic sources of meaning in life (as Blessing 2013: 116–17 points out), but they disagree over when and why they are. Both kinds of theorists also tend to agree on actions that lack meaning, with a very large majority concurring that the following confer no meaning on a life: chewing gum, taking a hot shower, watching sitcoms while eating ice cream, living the rest of one's life alone in a virtual reality (an 'experience machine', as many analytic philosophers call it, following Nozick 1974: 32–5), digging a hole and then filling it up and then digging a hole again and filling it up and so on indefinitely, killing one's innocent spouse for the insurance money, hating other people simply because of their race. *Some* of these actions are worth doing, but not because they would make one's life more significant. If one believes that some of these actions could do so, one has to tell a story that invokes some *further* condition, such as helping others or being rewarded for having made a sacrifice. Setting these kinds of conditions aside, the actions are widely taken to be meaningless for lacking the kinds of valuable properties mentioned earlier, or so most philosophers believe. The disagreement between them is instead mainly over precisely what is missing from such actions, and specifically whether (and how) spiritual conditions are relevant.

Note that if a group's existence were significant, there would not be any direct implication for the meaningfulness of the group's individual members, at least not by definition. Humanity's meaningfulness does not logically imply any particular human's meaningfulness. Similarly, if the lives of some persons were meaningful, it would not immediately follow that the human race as a whole is meaningful. So, the two enquiries are conceptually distinct, even if some philosophers believe that substantively they do influence each other.

There is some disagreement about whether one of these enquiries is primary or foundational in some way (for the minority view that the meaning of life is key, see Seachris 2009 and Tartaglia 2015), but this Element does not go into that matter in any depth. Instead, it usually addresses both enquiries side by side, while devoting somewhat more space to meaning in life since it has been the predominant focus of English-speaking philosophers for at least the past 100 years.

2.2 Conceptions of Life's Meaning

So far, this Section has sought to analyze the concept of life's meaning, or what is widely deemed uncontested amongst competing enquirers, viz., both those who favour spiritual accounts of it and those who do not. Now the Section turns to conceptions of life's meaning, that is, highly contested theories of what would constitute life's meaning.

Of key concern is how to distinguish religious from non-religious views. Here, the word 'supernaturalism' is used to connote accounts according to which God or a soul (or of course the pair) as standardly understood in the Jewish, Christian and Islamic faiths is central to making life (whether of the individual or of the group) meaningful. So, God is understood to be a perfect being, that is, a spiritual person beyond the realm of subatomic particles in (our) space–time who is the source of the universe and who is all-knowing, all-good and all-powerful. A soul is taken to be an immortal, spiritual substance that contains our identities and that will survive the deaths of our bodies. A supernaturalist is one who maintains that either God or a soul (or the pair) is central to life's meaning. At least one spiritual condition is deemed to be necessarily constitutive either of meaning as such or of a great meaning, where the relevant life is either that of an individual or of humanity.

Employing the term 'supernaturalism' is not meant to suggest that, for religiously oriented meaning theorists, the natural world is utterly irrelevant to making life meaningful (a concern expressed in Cottingham 2016a: 48–50). One might deem human beings to have been created in God's image, with meaning being constituted by how one treats them, for just one example. The term is instead meant to indicate that the physical world cannot confer much, if any, meaning in the absence of some connection with a spiritual dimension.

Naturalism is not quite simply the rejection of supernaturalism, because of the logical space for non-naturalism, the view that meaning is constituted by properties that are neither supernatural nor natural. Consider, for instance, the views of Immanuel Kant, insofar as he conceives of the highest good for finite persons in terms of the exercise of noumenal agency, which is neither a physical nor a spiritual property for him. A naturalist does reject supernaturalism, but further claims that physical properties are sufficient for a (greatly) meaningful life, whether of a person or of the species. The physical roughly consists of subatomic particles in our space–time and what is composed out of them, as is particularly well known through the scientific method.

2.3 Meaning and Metaphysics

Supernaturalism and naturalism are views about what would confer meaning on life. They are accounts of what would manifest a certain sort of value, and so are to be contrasted with metaphysical views, i.e., accounts of what exists. Theism is one such metaphysical view, and in the present context, it is the claim that something spiritual – characteristically God, but perhaps a soul on its own – exists, or that we can know such exists, while atheism here is the denial of theism. The term 'theism' is hereby used in this Element more broadly than is often the case; usually it is taken to mean the claim that God and a soul exist, or that God exists but not a soul, but here a possible variant of so-called theism is the claim that a soul exists but not God.

Most supernaturalists are theists, while most naturalists are atheists. That is, most of those who believe that the existence of God or a soul would alone make life's meaning possible or substantial also believe that the relevant spiritual conditions exist. And most of those who deny that the existence of God or a soul would alone make life's meaning possible or substantial also deny that these spiritual conditions exist.[4]

However, a supernaturalist could consistently be an atheist; one might think that God and a soul are necessary for life's meaning but deny that they exist, committing one to the 'nihilist' view that meaning is impossible for us. Albert Camus (1955) is famous for having held something like that combination of positions, as did Leo Tolstoy (1884), at least prior to having come to believe in God (albeit on faith). Similarly, one could be a naturalist who is a theist; there is no logical contradiction in holding that God and a soul exist, but that neither one is central to what makes life meaningful.

There is only a sparse literature addressing the competing likelihoods of the four combinations of views about meaning and metaphysics, viz., super-naturalism-theism, supernaturalism-atheism, naturalism-theism and naturalism-atheism. Although it is clear that philosophers most often cluster around the first

---

[4] Parts of the next two paragraphs have been cribbed from Metz (2019: 357–8).

and fourth positions, there is as yet little systematic discussion about whether they should.

One strategy to make headway that the field might consider is how metaphysical issues would affect the meta-ethical matter of 'where values come from'.[5] For example, if God does not exist, and the human species is merely a product of natural selection, then chances are that our value judgements, including those about meaning, arose because they enhanced fitness. And that function, in turn, probably did not depend on thought about a spiritual realm (see Metz 2013a: 242–4, 2016a: 74–6). For all we can tell, belief in God and a soul are relatively recent developments in human history and could not have influenced hominid evolution. Plus, the sort of perfection inherent to these concepts would have been unlikely to affect our reproduction in a world in which it does not exist; instead, imperfect standards achievable in a purely physical world would have most likely served the function of fostering human reproduction. This rationale suggests that in an atheist world, human beings would likely make naturalist judgements about meaningfulness, i.e., that the supernaturalist-atheist combination is implausible.

Conversely, if God existed and were the source of the universe, presumably He would also be the source of what is good for its own sake in it, including meaningfulness. In addition, He would do as much as He could to prompt us to become aware not merely of what is meaningful, but also of why it is. Hence, there is prima facie reason to believe that theism would support supernaturalism; even if it is not inconsistent to hold naturalism-theism, supernaturalism-theism might be more coherent.

These have been sketches of arguments, and not full-blown defences. However, they indicate how there might be theoretical leverage for favouring some of the four logically possible combinations of views about metaphysics and meaning as more substantively plausible than others. While that is of philosophical interest in its own right, it would also have an important bearing on our knowledge of what is meaningful, in the event we were confident about what exists. For example, if the supernaturalism-theism combination were shown to be more plausible than the naturalism-theism combination, and if we knew that theism were true, then there would be some evidence in favour of supernaturalism. These kinds of rationales are currently lacking sophisticated exploration in the field.

---

[5] For recent 'pro-theist' (and 'anti-theist') positions that are not squarely about life's meaning, but that consider the conceptual relationships between metaphysics and God's value (or disvalue), see Penner and Arbour (2018), Schellenberg (2018) and Tooley (2018).

3 Extreme Supernaturalism

For a long time in the history of Western philosophy, those who thought spiritual conditions are central to life's meaning tended to think that they are necessary for it. This latter, binary view is labelled an 'extreme' form of supernaturalism, for it entails that if neither God nor a soul exists, then humanity as a whole and individual human lives are all utterly meaningless.

A number of major philosophers from the medieval and modern periods held such a view. For Aquinas, the beatific vision, i.e., apprehending God without bodily distortion, is our final end; for Pascal, God is what alone can provide a sense of fulfilment, 'He only is our true good' (*Pensees* #425); for Kant, human persons could not achieve their highest good without the existence of both God and a soul; for Kierkegaard, faith in God is the only way to connect with the eternal and unchanging, essential for overcoming despair and finding meaning in one's life; for Tolstoy, life is not worth living if one lacks a soul and is destined to die along with one's body instead of to unite in paradise with God.

This Section spells out the major rationales for this version of supernaturalism, and indicates why contemporary philosophers have tended to doubt them. The aim is not to show that the arguments for extreme supernaturalism are indeed unconvincing, but to recount the history of the debate, with some suggestion about argumentative strategies that merit exploration in the twenty-first century.

When it is claimed that God, for instance, is 'necessary' for life's meaning, this is shorthand for 'identical to' it (in part). The claim is not merely that there would be no meaning without God, but rather that there would be no meaning without God because meaningfulness *essentially consists of* human life relating to God in a certain way. Hence, it will not support extreme supernaturalism to argue that because the universe would not exist without God having created it, there would be no human life at all and hence also no meaning either in or of human life. At best this reasoning would show that God is instrumentally necessary for life's meaning, i.e., that God is merely a means to the production of meaning, but this is not the relevant claim, which is instead that God must constitute life's meaning as an end.

Philosophers have presented five major arguments for the view that life's meaning is identical (in part) to God or a soul, which, in catchwords, appeal to God's purpose (3.1), relationality (3.2), an afterlife (3.3), humanity's origin (3.4) and humanity's prospects (3.5).[6] The first three concern meaning in life, the latter two the meaning of life.

---

[6] For other, less influential defences of extreme supernaturalism, see Hartshorne (1984), Smith (2000), Svenson (2000), Ellis (2011) and Metz (2013a: 119–22).

3.1 God's Purpose

The most influential argument for extreme supernaturalism about meaning in life is that a person's life is more meaningful, the more she fulfils a purpose that God has assigned to her. By this view, if God does not exist, or if He does but we fail to realize the end He has appointed us, then our lives are meaningless. By a 'simple' or 'pure' version of this view, it is just the fulfilment of the purpose that confers meaning, and not any gift or reward of eternal life in Heaven consequent to having done so (e.g. Brown 1971; Cottingham 2003).

There is of course disagreement about what God's purpose is (or would be, depending on one's metaphysics), with one major distinction being between those who believe His purpose is (or would be) universal in scope and others maintaining it is (or would be) particularized. The universalists are at home in the Christian and Islamic faiths, in which the same purposes of loving God and one's neighbour or glorifying God, respectively, are thought to have been assigned to all human persons. Amongst philosophers it has been common to hold that God's purpose would ground a universal moral system, one that applies to all human beings and that confers meaning on our lives when we live up to it (e.g. Cottingham 2005: 37–57; Craig 2013). In contrast, according to one strain of Judaism, (at least some) commandments from God as laid down in the Torah apply specifically to the Jewish people, and some philosophers believe that God would have to have a purpose unique to each individual in order to confer meaning on our lives (e.g. Affolter 2007; cf. Salles 2010).

The standard objection to a purpose-based account of why God is necessary for meaning is that not just any purpose assigned to us is intuitively meaning-conferring, and that it is the content of the purpose, not the fact that it has come from God, that makes it meaningful to fulfil or not. Consider, for example, the difference between serving as food for intergalactic travellers (Nagel 1971: 721; Nozick 1981: 586–7) or committing rape (Sinnott-Armstrong 2009: 106), on the one hand, and donating money to the poor, on the other. If God were to assign the former purposes to human beings, they would not confer meaning on our lives, or so most readers will think. If not, then the mere fact that God is the source of a purpose is not what makes it meaningful; it is rather what the purpose would have us do, making the fact that it has come from God irrelevant.

This standard objection now has a standard reply, which involves two claims. First, the point is made that God could not assign a purpose that would intuitively fail to confer meaning when we fulfil it since its content would be fixed by His inherent nature as beneficent, loving, just or more generally all-good. 'Since God is perfectly good, his purposes for human life will assuredly have positive value' (Quinn 2000: 59; see also Cottingham 2005: 46–9, 2016b: 127–8).

This move, if it works, is sufficient to show that God's purpose would not fail to have the intuitively right sort of content. However, an additional move must be made in order to show that this content would have to come from God. Otherwise, it would remain open to maintain that, while God's purpose for us could be one source of meaning in our lives, it is not necessary for meaning since a purpose with the right content could come from another source.

So, second, the point is made that God, as a being with the highest degree of compossible perfections (final goods), could be the only source of values that are higher than what can be found in the experience of pleasures or the satisfaction of desires (Craig 2009a, 2009b, 2013; Cottingham 2005: 52–6; Poettcker 2015). Where could objective and superlative values, ones transcending the contingencies of sensation and conation found in the animal kingdom, come from? A strong answer is: God's nature as all-good, all-knowing and all-powerful. That is the deep explanation proffered of why the good, the true and the beautiful, all of which involve the exercise of rationality, are exemplars of meaning; for earthly realities are meaningful only insofar as they 'participate in' or 'reflect' the logos of divine idealities. For example, our lives become more meaningful by acting morally in certain ways just because it is God's beneficence that grounds an objective system of rules applying to all human beings; when we perform great moral deeds, we are thereby doing something of what we can to realize what is divine within us.

In sum, the main argument for extreme supernaturalism is that God's nature could alone be the source of values beyond animal nature, where His purposes for us would be informed by His nature, and would probably amount to having us be as godlike – roughly, beneficent, knowledgeable and creative – as we can, given our limitations. What makes a way of life meaningless, then, is that it is inconsistent with the sort of purpose that God could assign in the light of His perfect essence. 'The theist can agree that God forbids rape because it is bad; and it is bad because it is incompatible with God's nature' (Craig 2009b: 173). If God did not exist, then rape would not be bad, and, indeed, there would be no distinction between the moral and the immoral, or the meaningful and the meaningless, by this view.

Many in the field accept the point that meaning in life would be higher than what a typical animal's life could exhibit (set aside the likes of chimpanzees and dolphins, for now), but question whether such a value would have to come from God. Of particular relevance is a naturalist realism, according to which final goods are constituted by mind-independent, physical properties.

To illustrate this alternative conception of value, consider what it is to be healthy. It appears to be good for its own sake (despite clearly also being an instrumental good). It would be unwise to sacrifice, say, mental health for the sake of subjective, animal values; being addicted or experiencing mania could conceivably bring long-term pleasure and desire satisfaction in their wake, but doing so would be unattractive, on balance. And it does not seem necessary to reach for God in order to understand what makes a human organism healthy or not; the properties that biologists and psychologists empirically study will suffice.

In sum, being healthy appears to be an objective property that is highly valuable and that is not essentially constituted by facts about God. If we can identify one such property, why not think there are more? In particular, why not think that meaningfulness is similar to healthiness?[7] Instead of beneficence, knowledge and creativity being identical to God's nature, perhaps they could exist as meaningful in nature without God.

Although this option is now familiar to the field, it has hardly commanded widespread acceptance (for just two sceptics in the context of meaning literature, see Cottingham 2008: 267, and Blessing 2013: 115–17). This debate, about how objective value is possible, has been flourishing since the 1980s, and resolving it will require substantial engagements in not just axiology,[8] but also metaphysics, epistemology and language.

3.2 Relationality

A second major argument for extreme supernaturalism, regarding God's necessity for meaning in our lives, appeals to the idea that meaningfulness in general seems to be essentially relational (Nozick 1981: 594–618). What a word means is a function of a referential relationship with something in the world, and when smoke is said to 'mean' fire, there is a causal relationship involved between two events. When we now consider the meaning in a human life, it too appears to be relational, such that any meaningful condition in it has obtained its meaning from something beyond it.

For example, a person's life is presumably meaningful in virtue of helping others, knowing certain theories or creating artworks. Other people, theories and artworks are beyond a given person and confer meaning on her life when

---

[7] Moral realists routinely invoke healthiness to show that it is possible for there to be a naturalist objective good, with rightness or virtue analogous to it. For an overview, see Lutz and Lenman (2018).

[8] For one issue to be hashed out, consider Wielenberg's (2005: 48–50) contention that grounding all value in God's purpose is incompatible with acknowledging the reality of intrinsic goodness, something that is good for its own sake in virtue of its non-relational properties.

she is related to them in the right way. But now the suggestion is that these external conditions, or their relationships with the person, also must themselves obtain their meaning from something beyond them. '[W]e have a tendency to ask by what further criteria a goal or purpose that is meant to bestow meaning is itself meaningful. For any end point or limit we reach, there seems the possibility of moving past it, which puts it into question' (Waghorn 2014: 3). Specifically, perhaps the theories about X are meaningful for having a bearing on other intellectual matters Y, and the artworks, when viewed, are meaningful insofar as they are going to broaden people's horizons in significant ways. And, then, *these* external conditions must, in turn, get their meaning or point from something beyond them and so on, until the regress is terminated in an all-encompassing, unconditioned condition for all other meaningful conditions. That is God (for this argument, see especially Nozick 1981: 594–610, and Bennett-Hunter 2014).

The logic of this argument entails that without an unlimited source, there would be no limited sorts of meaning. That is so, since, for any limited sort of meaning, it must obtain its meaning from something external to it. Setting aside the idea of circular support or an infinite regress, there must be a foundation with nothing external to it that either uniquely has an intrinsic meaning or is beyond considerations of meaning altogether. This ultimate source of meaning in the universe is plausibly identified as God, so the argument goes.

Whether this conception of God could be the one championed by the Judeo-Christian-Islamic tradition raises tricky issues. Proponents of the relational argument often maintain that the unlimited source of all meaning would have to be ineffable (Nozick 1981: 608; Cooper 2003: 126–42; Bennett-Hunter 2014, 2016; Waghorn 2014; cf. Nagel 1987: 99), which appears incompatible with the thought that it is a spiritual person with the 'omni-properties'. It is not clear, in short, that relationality about meaning supports supernaturalism of the sort discussed in this Element.

Suppose, though, that God's unlimitedness can be shown to be compatible with the more usual suspects when it comes to perfections. Let us instead consider not whether the unlimited source of all meaning counts as 'God', but rather whether for a condition to be meaningful it must ultimately be grounded on an unlimited source of all meaning. It *does* always seem sensible to ask for the point of any finite meaningful condition. However, being able to enquire intelligibly into the meaning beyond a meaningful condition does not necessarily show that the latter would not have its meaning were it not for the former.[9] That is, a meaningful condition might have more meaning for being connected

---

[9] Some of the following analysis has been borrowed from Metz (2016b: 1251–2).

in the right way with something beyond it, even if it would retain some meaning if it were not so connected.

For example, it appears meaningful to overcome an addiction or a neurosis. Doing so is plausibly a matter of transcending one's animal self, having done something in which to take great pride or grounding a compelling story about one's life. Now, one can, with the relational theorist, indeed ask what the point of doing so is, with a good answer being that, having improved one's mental health, one could then help others to a much greater extent, which would be meaningful. However, while helping others would surely confer *more* meaning on having improved one's mental health, one need not maintain, as the relational theorist would, that there would be *no* meaning whatsoever if one did not do that (or something like it). There would plausibly be some meaning in having successfully struggled to overcome mental illness *in itself*, even though there would be more if that were to have good consequences for others.

In sum, the challenge to the relational theorist is that meaning might be essentially relational without being exhaustively so. If there is an intrinsic dimension to meaningfulness, as the mental health case suggests, then a regress on meaningful conditions might reveal merely how much meaning is possible for a given condition, not what the ultimate possibility for that condition to be at all meaningful is. This is a challenge to the relational rationale for extreme supernaturalism that needs to be addressed.[10]

3.3 An Afterlife

The first two arguments for extreme supernaturalism have focused on God, without reference to a soul, while the conclusion of the next one instead posits a soul as essentially constitutive of meaning. The next rationale implies that, even if God exists, a relationship with Him would be insufficient for meaning in the absence of one's enjoying eternal life upon the death of one's body.

In fact, this reasoning is present in what is likely the very first written work in the monotheist tradition to address considerations of meaning explicitly, namely, the book of Ecclesiastes in the Hebrew Bible. A plain reading of the text, now more than 2,000 years old, suggests the view that 'all is futility' (1.2) and that 'all the happenings beneath the sun' are akin to 'the pursuit of wind' (1.14), because we are sure to perish along with the inevitable deaths of our

---

[10] For a reply, see Bennett-Hunter (2016: 1280–1). Another criticism is to accept that meaning is exhaustively relational, but to deny that a condition must obtain its meaning from another meaningful condition. Nozick himself, upon reflection, maintains that a condition could obtain meaning insofar as it is related to something finally valuable that is not itself meaningful (1981: 610; see also Thomson 2003: 25–6).

bodies. The author of the text clearly accepts that God exists, but also clearly states:

> [I]n respect of the fate of man and the fate of beast, they have one and the same fate: as the one dies so dies the other, and both have the same lifebreath; man has no superiority over beast, since both amount to nothing. (3.19)

Without a soul, we cannot transcend the values of the animal kingdom for the author of Ecclesiastes, who remarks, 'I decided, as regards men, to dissociate them [from] the divine beings and to face the fact that they are beasts' (3.18), and who maintains that the only thing worth doing for a mortal person is 'to eat and drink and enjoy himself' (8.15). The higher value of meaning is unavailable to those who will die (for more recent adherents to this view, see Tolstoy 1884; Morris 1992; Craig 2013; Haught 2013).

It is worth pressing to ask *why* death is sufficient for there being 'no real value under the sun' (2.11). Sometimes the claim is that it is meaningless for good people to face the same fate as the wicked, where the latter deserve to die (Ecclesiastes 2.14–2.16, 9.2–9.3). Other times, the thought is that nothing is worth doing unless it will have some ultimate consequence for oneself or the universe (Tolstoy 1884). Still other times, the suggestion is that meaning depends on moral perfection, which would require an eternity to develop (Kant's *Critique of Practical Reason*). More recently, some have suggested that, insofar as a meaningful life is a worthwhile one, a worthwhile life would only be one that enjoyed happiness for all eternity (Goetz 2012).

A problem common to all four of these rationales is that, while they provide prima facie support for the claim that immortality is necessary for meaning, they do not uniquely ground a particular, spiritual form of it.[11] If the universe were spatio-temporally infinite, then one could conceivably be immortal in a purely physical world. It appears that one need not have a soul in order to avoid the deserved fate of the wicked, to see one's life make an ultimate difference, to perfect one's virtue or to partake of eternal bliss.

Although it might be true that it 'has been the view of most people that a necessary condition for the survival of death is that one be or have a soul that is separate from its physical body and capable of surviving the demise of the latter' (Goetz 2012: 23), the philosophical grounds for this view are shaky – just imagine the contents of one's mind being uploaded into a computer and then downloaded into successive bodies forever.[12] That appears no less promising a route to an afterlife than the contents of one's mind being contained in

---

[11] Setting aside criticisms of particular instances, which are of course available.

[12] For thorough analyses of how physical immortality might be metaphysically possible, see Baker (2017) and Steinhart (2017).

a spiritual substance. In principle, immortality could be realized in either a theist or an atheist world (granting that we human beings probably cannot bring our immortality about in this particular world).

For a proper defence of extreme supernaturalism, there has to be a plausible explanation of why a spiritual immortality is necessary for meaning in life, and why a physical one would be insufficient for it. A promising position is that, without a soul, we could not come close to God in the way that is required for a significant existence. Given God's inherently spiritual nature, if we are to commune with Him in a robust and hence meaning-conferring way, we must shed our physical selves and engage with Him on a spiritual plane alone. In short, meeting our maker would involve transcendence and constitute a good life-story, where a proper meeting of the minds could take place only if we were disembodied. This widely held position harks back particularly to Aquinas in the tradition of Western philosophy (examples of contemporary philosophical adherents include Davis 1987, Craig 2013 and Mawson 2016: 155, 178).[13]

At this stage of the dialectic, much turns on how much higher the value of meaning is relative to animal goods and whether perfection is essential to it. The present conception of meaning involves the existence of a perfect being who is ultimately responsible for our having been created, where meaning consists of being in a perfect relationship with Him, namely, returning to God in the form of an intense union with Him that lasts forever in Heaven. Let us grant, at this point, that this would be ideal.[14] Why think that meaning in life is constituted only by what is ideal?

One reason for thinking that it is not is that meaning intuitively comes in degrees; some lives have, or at least could have, more meaning in them than others that also have some. However, if the maximally conceivable or possible value, viz., the perfect way of relating to a perfect being, is alone constitutive of meaning, then it appears that everyone's life is either equally meaningful or meaningless, with no one having more meaning in his life than someone else who also does have some meaning. According to this conception, meaningfulness is either one or zero, with nothing in between.

One might reply that, by the present image, some could come closer to God than others, based on what they did during their early lives, which would account for degrees of meaning. However, it is not clear that there would be differential degrees of meaning, given an infinite amount of time for all the lives in touch with God. Infinity multiplied by any positive number is infinity, after

---

[13] This approach is incompatible with the strand of Christianity according to which the faithful can look forward to bodily resurrection. Friends of that view will likely try to argue that a soul is necessary in order for one's self to survive the death of one's present body.

[14] Section 6 provides prima facie grounds for doubting that it would be ideal.

all. Plus, making this move, which amounts to allowing for a less than perfect relationship with a perfect being, seems to undercut the motivation for positing God and a soul as necessary for meaning in the first place, which is that only perfection is high enough to ground the value of meaning.

Additional concerns about the relevance of perfection are considered later in this Element (especially Section 4). For now, let us turn to two remaining rationales for extreme supernaturalism. The first three concerned meaning in life, that is, the respects in which an individual person's life may or may not be meaningful, while the conclusion of the last two is about the meaning of human life as such.

3.4 Humanity's Origin

Recall that debate about the meaning 'of' life is about how a higher-order purpose, a transcending of animal values or a compelling life-story (or other properties that many associate with meaning-talk by definition) might be realized by the human species. One argument appeals to humanity's past, while another invokes its future.

The past-oriented argument in the philosophical literature is that God is necessary for humanity to be meaningful insofar as only He could have created it in the relevant way. William Lane Craig, the influential Christian philosopher, advances a version of this argument:

> Without God the universe is the result of a cosmic accident, a chance explosion. There is no reason for which it exists. As for man, he is a freak of nature – a blind product of matter plus time plus chance. Man is just a lump of slime that evolved into rationality. There is no more purpose in life for the human race than for a species of insect; for both are the result of the blind interaction of chance and necessity. (2013: 162–3; see also Gordon 1983; Cottingham 2003: 35–48; cf. Mawson 2016: 64–6; Swinburne 2016: 154)

One idea the passage suggests is that life would be meaningless without God, and specifically His purpose for human beings as a whole, because without it no one has intended that we exist. One might buttress this reasoning by appealing to the idea that for anything to have a meaning, a prior purposive agent must have ascribed it a point or significance (Morris 1992: 56–7). Since humanity was of course not present in order to ascribe its own creation a point, it must have been an agent external to humanity, God.

However, even if, *per argumentum*, our life as a species would be meaningful just insofar as it had been created by some other agent with a purpose for us, no reason has been given yet for thinking that God must have been the prior agent. For that additional point, it is tempting to suggest that our creation was meaningful insofar as it came from a well-meaning source. What is at stake when it comes to the reasons for humanity's creation is perhaps 'whether or not they were positively evaluable intentional states. That is why evolution is felt to be so threatening to our meaningfulness, both to us as a species and (thus) to us as individuals' (Mawson 2016: 65).

Yet this is not quite enough either, for we can imagine benevolent aliens with weaker powers than God having created the human species for certain ends. What the supernaturalist needs to provide is some reason for thinking that only God could have been a meaning-conferring creator.

Here are some possibilities. Perhaps we are led back to the idea that only having sprung from a perfect being would be a truly significant antecedent to our existence. Or it might be that it is important to have a 'place in an appropriate larger scheme of things (God's plan)' (Mawson 2016: 65), one for the universe as a whole that perhaps only its creator could have assigned. Or maybe it is something about having been produced by a necessary being and so being inherent to the fabric of reality that matters (cf. Trisel 2012: 400; Metz 2013a: 83–4; Seachris 2013: 14). Or yet another thought is that only God could have produced us to cohere with the rest of the universe that, as a whole, fits together so as to manifest an aesthetic unity (Gordon 1983). The field has yet to hash out these options in a thorough way.

Regardless of the exact reason for thinking that having been created only by God would be sufficient for the meaning of life, there are at least two major concerns for this position. One is an analogical objection to the idea that humanity's source is crucial to its meaningfulness. Just as an individual person's life can be meaningful, even if his parents had created him accidentally, so the life of the species can be meaningful, even if it had arisen by chance. Consider, for instance, the life of Albert Einstein, often taken to be an exemplar of meaningfulness in the philosophical literature. 'In judging whether his life was meaningful, no one would ever ask "Was his existence intended?"' (Trisel 2012: 400). By analogy, if the existence of the human race as a whole can be significant, it is probably not its origin that is essentially at stake.

Here is a second reason for doubting that humanity's source is the key to its meaning. Suppose that the human race had been created by God, where such creation is alone constitutive of its meaning. In that case, there would be nothing to be done on the part of humanity in respect of its being meaningful. No matter what human beings were to do, considered as a collective, humanity would be meaningful for having been created by the right agent and for the right purpose. However, most enquirers into life's meaning, including into the meaning of the human race, believe that what is crucially at stake is what shape that life should take upon having come into existence. Merely having sprung from a certain source and for a certain reason, even if that confers *some* meaning on the human race, is not enough to judge it to be meaningful on balance, so the objection goes.

3.5 Humanity's Prospects

The last rationale for extreme supernaturalism, and in respect of the meaning of life, avoids these two objections to the previous rationale. Instead of focusing on our past when it comes to the meaning of human life, it directs us towards our future. According to the fifth influential argument for thinking that God or a soul is necessary for life's meaning, it comes, roughly, from good triumphing over evil in the universe or the redemption of suffering in it.

A particularly powerful version of this view would be combined with the previous one, so that what is meaningful for humanity is having been assigned such a purpose by God and then having done what it takes to fulfil it (Davis 1987; Walker 1989; Craig 2009b: 183, 2013; Seachris 2016). That is, there would be a meaningful narrative to the human race, a story with a beginning, a middle and an end. The beginning would amount to having been created by God, not merely in order to honour or to love Him, but also to promote goodness in His universe. The middle would be a time of conflict and struggle, when human beings grapple with their weaknesses and strive to overcome evil, both personal and impersonal. The end need not be understood as death, but rather as having helped to realize a noble aim for which the universe was created and then, consequent to that achievement, perhaps having entered Heaven and thereby forever returned to humanity's source of a just and loving God.

Most critics of supernaturalism have been naturalists who have focused on meaning in life, thinking that, while the human race is probably incapable of being meaningful, individual human lives still can be meaningful. Explicit naturalist proposals about what could make the human species meaningful are sparse. However, two types of suggestions in the recent philosophical literature merit consideration as ways of doubting that God or a soul must exist in order for the human species to have a point in virtue of its future.

Here is one idea, from Brooke Alan Trisel, who has most directly addressed the issue of late:

> By engaging with inherently valuable and natural goods, it adds meaning to our individual lives which, in turn, adds meaning to humanity from the 'bottom-up'. As more individual lives become meaningful, there is a corresponding increase in the meaning of human life. (2016: 3)

By this 'aggregated' approach (Trisel 2016: 10), the more that human persons were to participate in projects that involve love, wisdom, beauty and the like, the more that it would be plausible to say that humanity as such has a significant existence, at least upon a time when most humans live in this way.

In contrast, a second sort of naturalist proposal about how humanity's existence could be meaningful is more collective, focused on what the group qua group might achieve. So, if human beings, perhaps through some organization such as the United Nations, were to strive collaboratively to overcome poverty, unemployment, oppression and discrimination, these achievements would be properly ascribed to humanity, or at least to it at a certain point in time. For another example, if many countries around the world cooperated in order to meet another intelligent species in the universe (proposed as a potent source of meaning by Mulgan 2015: 321–2, 330, 361; cf. Nozick 1981: 618), then, again, meaning would plausibly accrue to a group that far transcends an individual person.

The careful reader will have noticed some hedging in these naturalist approaches to the meaning of life. In particular, they seem to ground the claim that humanity *at a certain stage* would be meaningful, not so much that the human species, as something stretching over millions of years, would be. Are these 'revisionary' naturalist suggestions about how humanity as something beyond an individual person could obtain meaning sufficient, or is there the firm intuition that it is the species in its entirety that has, or is at least capable of, meaning? The field currently lacks systematic discussion of precisely how to conceive of humanity as a potential bearer of meaning.

Another concern about the naturalist approaches to the meaning of life is that they do not seem to ground narratives as compelling as the supernaturalist one broadly sketched earlier in this Element. They cannot account for the desirability of humanity having sprung from a certain, caring source that grounds the universe. They lack any connection with a grand plan for everything that exists. They are consistent with the eventual death of the human species, an unwelcome ending.

On this score, one could grant that the supernaturalist narrative would be *better* than its naturalist rivals – perhaps even that it provides 'the best story we have about life's meanings' (Quinn 2000: 66) – but deny the extreme supernaturalist judgement that there would be *no* meaning in the naturalist ones. Most would say that human beings indeed ought to come together to fight injustice on the globe and to meet intelligent life beyond it, where a plausible explanation of why is that doing so would confer some meaning on humanity. These would be good stories to tell about the human race, ones meriting the reaction of pride. If so, then it is implausible to think that humanity can be meaningful only if God has assigned it a certain purpose, it has fulfilled the purpose and God has rewarded or otherwise responded positively to it for having done so.

However, a moderate supernaturalism is still in the cards – perhaps the supernaturalist story would alone confer a much greater meaning on humanity than what any naturalist one could (cf. Section 5).

4 Moderate Naturalism

In the previous Section, five major arguments for extreme supernaturalism were expounded and evaluated. Although criticisms of these arguments were presented, extreme supernaturalism itself was not directly challenged. This Section considers reasons for denying that God or a soul is necessary for life's meaning, and for thinking that it would be possible in a purely physical world. This latter claim is labelled 'moderate naturalism' since it is consistent with the idea that a spiritual dimension could enhance the meaning in or of life.

This Section first fleshes out what naturalism in respect of life's meaning involves in more detail than has been done up to now (4.1), after which it addresses three arguments for it. One is that supernaturalism cannot avoid being unintelligible (4.2), a second is that many would have inconsistent beliefs if they held supernaturalism (4.3) and a third, which is the most influential, is that meaning in life appears intuitively possible in an atheist world (4.4).

4.1 The Nature of Naturalism

What do naturalists tend to believe would be meaningful in life, if atheism were true? Supernaturalists sometimes suggest that naturalists are invariably subjectivists who contend that what is meaningful varies from person to person or group to group, depending on whatever they happen to want, believe or choose (e.g. Cottingham 2005: 53; Craig 2013: 161, 167). There have of course been naturalists who are subjectivists, and most probably were for much of the twentieth century (e.g. Sartre 1956; Frankfurt 1988; Ayer 2000; Taylor 2000: 319–34). However, most naturalists these days reject subjectivism because of its counterintuitive implications about what can count as a meaningful life. Subjectivism oddly entails that if one really desired 'cultivating one's prowess at long-distance spitting or collecting a big ball of string' (Wolf 2010: 104), or spending one's entire life alone in an experience machine, then one's life would be quite meaningful for doing so.

Instead, much more popular amongst naturalists over the past thirty years has been some kind of objectivism, according to which there are certain ways of being and doing that humans have reasons of meaning to want, to deem important or to choose if they currently do not. By this approach, if you strongly desire to collect a big ball of string and succeed in orienting your life towards that project, no meaning will accrue to your life. You should change your desires and choices in order for meaning to arise, focusing instead on, say, creating a family, getting an education or writing poetry.

Most commonly held is the sort of view captured by Susan Wolf's pithy slogan: 'Meaning arises when subjective attraction meets objective attractiveness' (2010: 62). This theory, which obviously includes both subjective and objective elements, implies that no meaning accrues to one's life if one desires, believes in or chooses a project that is not worthwhile, or if one engages in a worthwhile project but fails to like it, judges it to be unimportant or has been forced to undertake it. Different versions of this theory will have different accounts of the appropriate mental states and of worthwhileness.

Wolf herself eschews the search for a common denominator to all the worthwhile projects, as have other naturalists who maintain there is an irreducible pluralism amongst objectively meaningful conditions (e.g. Kekes 2000). However, most party to the debate accept that the good, the true and the beautiful are at least exemplars of these conditions; roughly, morality, enquiry and creativity are routinely identified as representative naturalist sources of meaning in life. And, then, some have sought to identify a single physical property that might underlie this classic triad and any other sources of meaning, with proposals including (amongst others) that one's life is objectively meaningful insofar as it: is creative (Taylor 1987); promotes theoretical and practical rationality in exceptional ways (Smith 1997: 179–221); realizes goals that are transcendent for being long-lasting in duration and broad in scope (Mintoff 2008); or contours one's rational nature towards fundamental conditions of human existence (Metz 2013a: 199–239).

4.2 Unintelligibility

The rest of this Section supposes that some kind of objectivism not merely is the most influential amongst naturalists in the twenty-first century, but also poses the strongest naturalist challenge to supernaturalism. In the literature, there have been three major ways that philosophers have sought to show that no spiritual condition is necessary for life's meaning, whereas some objective physical condition (perhaps in combination with a subjective one) is sufficient for it.[15]

One way that naturalists have sought to provide reason to reject any supernaturalist theory of life's meaning is to contend that it is, upon reflection, unintelligible. There is a weaker and a stronger version of this argument. The weaker version is the somewhat familiar claim that God and a soul are difficult

---

[15] For some newer arguments that have yet to be taken up, see Megill and Linford (2016: 36–41), and then for arguments that spiritual conditions are not merely unnecessary for life's meaning, but also would reduce it, see Section 6.

to understand. For example, in one of the first book-length analytic treatments of life's meaning, Irving Singer says of speaking of 'God's purpose' that

> to talk in this way is to assume that one can refer to an intentionality outside of time and space comparable to what occurs within. That is the basic flaw in the analogy ... It is not a question of determining whether we can fathom the cosmic plan, or prove that a cosmic planner exists, or manage to fulfill his purposive program. It is a question of knowing whether our mind is able to formulate these notions with any degree of clarity. (Singer 1996: 31–2; see also Nagel 1987: 99; Hepburn 2000: 223)

A quick way to respond would be to maintain that God's eternality means not that He would be outside of time altogether, but rather inside it forever. Presumably, though, other facets of God would be hard to grasp, given His spiritual nature as so radically different from what we are normally acquainted with during our lives on earth.

The stronger version of the argument is not that God and a soul are unintelligible, but that they must be insofar as they are deemed to be necessary for life's meaning (Metz 2013b). The claim is that the logic of supernaturalism as a theory of meaning requires spiritual conditions to be quite different from what exists in the physical world and hence to be beyond what we can conceive. On the one hand, in order for God (or a soul) to be the sole source of meaning, God must be utterly unlike us. The more God were like us, the more reason there would be to think we could obtain meaning from ourselves, absent God. On the other hand, the more God were utterly unlike us and radically other, perhaps for being atemporal or absolutely simple, the less clear it would be whether we could truly understand His nature or how we could obtain meaning by relating to Him.

One familiar type of reply is to maintain that, with effort, we can in fact conceive what is radically other than us. Philosophers and theologians have made efforts to put themselves in God's shoes, and, for instance, have indeed been able to convey what it would be like to be outside of (our) time, viz., by viewing (our) time as a line with a past, present and future and then stepping back, perpendicular to it, and seeing the line all at once.

A newer and particularly intriguing sort of reply is to welcome the idea that only the ineffable could in fact ground meaning in our lives (Cooper 2003: 126–42; Bennett-Hunter 2014, 2016; Waghorn 2014). Invoking the relational conception of meaning discussed earlier (3.2), the thought is that for anything in a human life to obtain meaning, it must flow from a source that transcends the human altogether and that is beyond what we can in principle articulate or conceive. A prominent advocate of this approach is Guy Bennett-Hunter, who remarks:

> Life is itself meaningful in virtue of being experienced as being in a relation
> of appropriateness to what is beyond itself. And it is only as determinately
> meaningless that what is beyond the human can, in a non-circular manner,
> function as the measure for all human meanings ... [T]he measure must be
> undiscursable, ineffable: in short, a *mystery*. (2014: 124, 27)

Instead of meaning coming from what is intelligible, it can come only from what
is inconceivable, by this relational approach.

One issue here is of course whether the relational conception of meaning is
correct, and specifically whether we must connect with what is indeterminate
and incomprehensible in order for our lives, as individuals or as a species, to
have meaning. Another issue, though, is whether what is indeterminate and
incomprehensible even could in principle confer any meaning. One might have
thought not, insofar as a life is meaningful for being intelligible or making
sense – and is so by definition for some thinkers (e.g. Thomson 2003: 8–13;
Seachris 2016; cf. Affolter 2007: 445–50). Might it be possible for God to be
unintelligible while the meaning that inheres in a relationship with Him is
intelligible, or would the ineffability of the *relatum*, viz., God, remove the
prospect of the sense-making of the relationship of which He were a part (cf.
Bennett-Hunter 2016: 1277–80)?

4.3 Incoherence

Another strategy by which to cast doubt on the view that a spiritual realm is
necessary for life's meaning has been to contend that many of those inclined to
hold the view would evince an incoherence in doing so, as it would be in tension
with claims they already hold, or at least sensibly should (Metz 2013a: 87–97).
The target, here, is not quite supernaturalism as such so much as supernaturalists, who tend to hold certain additional claims inconsistent with it, or would be
reasonable to.

Specifically, if a supernaturalist claims to *know that meaning exists* (either
at the individual or at the species level), as most do, and then if she also claims
not to know that a spiritual realm exists (even if she has faith in it), as many do
and should, then she would be contradicting herself to claim to *know that if
meaning exists, then a spiritual realm exists* (a principle implied by extreme
supernaturalism). Consider each clause.

First, we plausibly have evidence sufficient for knowledge that human lives
are meaningful in some way. Or at least a very large majority of supernaturalists
believe that they know that some actions have meaning (loving one's neighbour
as oneself) and that others do not (long-distance spitting).

Second, although we have enough evidence to know that meaningfulness
exists, we probably do not have such in respect of God or a soul. Relatively few

contemporary philosophers debate about whether meaning exists, with most of the disagreements being about its source and nature, whereas, in contrast, there is quite a lot of debate amongst them about whether God or a soul exists, even if religiously inclined ones believe in them on faith. The presence of substantial disagreement amongst experts about whether spiritual conditions exist suggests a lack of conclusive evidence that they do exist.

The combination of these two claims renders it incoherent to believe that God's or a soul's existence is necessary for human lives to be meaningful. If we know that meaning exists, but do not know that God or a soul exists, then it would be contradictory to claim to know that if meaning exists, then God or a soul exists (extreme supernaturalism).

Critics have made a variety of replies to this argument against extreme supernaturalism, most often contending that there is in fact knowledge of God, that there is conclusive evidence, and not mere faith, for the supernaturalist to access. Indeed, some have suggested that there is *now* knowledge that God exists, given that there is meaning in human lives and that meaning implies God existence (e.g. Waghorn 2015: 159–60; Cottingham 2016a: 52; Wielenberg 2016: 29[16]).

4.4 Counterintuitiveness

The last salient argument against extreme supernaturalism has been the most common one for naturalists to make, and it is less complicated than the other two. It is the contention that meaning, at least in life, intuitively seems possible despite atheism, even when such meaning is construed objectively and not merely subjectively.

If we think of the stereotypical lives of Mother Teresa, Albert Einstein and Pablo Picasso, they seem meaningful merely in virtue of the activities they performed, even if we suppose there is no all-good, all-knowing and all-powerful spiritual person who is the ground of the universe and who will grant eternal bliss to our spiritual selves upon the deaths of our bodies (Trisel 2004: 384–5; Wielenberg 2005: 31–7, 49–50, 2016: 31, 33–4; Norman 2006). Supposing for the sake of argument we are currently living in an atheist world, we remain inclined to differentiate between lives devoted to long-distance spitting, creating a big ball of string or living in an experience machine, on the one hand, and those exemplifying morality, enquiry or creativity, on the other. Meaning is absent in the former cases and present in the latter ones, which can constitute ends higher than pleasure that merit pride or admiration upon their realization.

---

[16] For responses to these critics, see Metz (2015: 258–62, 2016a: 69–74).

The argument is powerful, having convinced even many religiously inclined theorists of meaning. For example, one has said that it is 'beyond reasonable doubt' that some meaning would be possible even if there were no God and a soul (Quinn 2000: 58), while another remarks that it would be 'incredible' (Audi 2005: 334) to think that no meaning would accrue from beneficent relationships in themselves. A recurrent example is rescuing a young girl from severe injury; surely, that would be a meaningful deed to perform, even if a perfect being does not exist and we will die along with the inevitable demise of our bodies, so the argument goes (Trisel 2004: 384–5; Audi 2005: 341–2).

It is possible that some supernaturalists will have contrary intuitions, especially those who maintain that any non-subjective goods or values higher than what is animal must have their source in God's nature (e.g. Cottingham 2005: 37–57; Craig 2013; Poettcker 2015: 200–1). In fact, Tolstoy does at one point question whether he should guard his children since they will die (1884: chapter 4; cf. Craig 2009b: 184). And, more theoretically, one might suggest that we are disposed to find meaning in morality, enquiry and creativity only because these values have sprung from an all-good, all-knowing and all-powerful person, such that if we suppose there is no God and are really clear about what that involves, then there is no superlative value of meaning to be had from the classic triad. Naturalists retort that the direction of influence goes the other way around: our concept of God is an idealized extrapolation from our highest earthly values, which came first.

In any event, a more common response from religious thinkers to the present objection has been to drop an extreme approach to supernaturalism and to opt for a moderate one. That is, many have explicitly granted that *some* meaning would be possible without God or a soul, characteristically through the good, the true and the beautiful, but have maintained that only spiritual conditions could provide a much *greater* meaning, a view discussed in the following Section.

5 Moderate Supernaturalism

Although one does continue to encounter in the twenty-first century some arguments for extreme supernaturalism, what is salient is the development of a new cluster of positions that do not imply that a world without God and a soul must completely lack meaning. Instead, there is often an acknowledgement that a purely physical world could ground some meaning in life (if not meaning of life), combined with the claim that a spiritual dimension is alone what could provide life a 'great' or 'ultimate' meaning.

After expounding this moderate supernaturalism (5.1), this Section critically discusses three major arguments for it in respect of meaning in life recently advanced in the literature, specifically, those that appeal to an afterlife (5.2), to becoming part of God's life (5.3) and to the satisfaction of our deepest desires (5.4).[17] The Section concludes by raising a problem common to all three rationales, that if they provide reason to believe a spiritual dimension would alone provide the ability for life to matter greatly, they provide comparable reason to believe a spiritual dimension would alone provide the ability for life to 'anti-matter' greatly (5.5).

5.1 The Concept of a Great Life's Meaning

To begin to appreciate the prominence of moderate supernaturalism, consider these recent titles: *Is Goodness without God Good Enough?* (Garcia and King 2009) and 'How God Makes Life a Lot More Meaningful' (Swinburne 2016). The phrasings imply that life could be good or meaningful, respectively, without God, but that it would be lacking the degree of goodness or meaning available only in a world in which He exists.

Sometimes the acknowledgement of some naturalist meaning is explicit, as when T. J. Mawson remarks about the extreme version of supernaturalism:

> [I]f we are in fact in a Godless universe, everyone's life – from that led by Gandhi to that led by that wastrel youth who lives at the other end of your street ... is entirely meaningless. Gandhi and the wastrel each score a flat zero. But that is a hard teaching. Who can believe it? ... [I]t might well be true that Gandhi's life is more meaningful than that of the wastrel even if there is no God. But, if there is no God, then there's some deeper or more permanent sort of meaning that even Gandhi's life lacked because *all* our lives lack it. (2016: 5; see also 17)

Here, the language is not the quantitative one of 'more' meaning or of whether there is 'enough' of it; it instead speaks of a meaning that is 'deep' or 'permanent',[18] as opposed to a 'shallow or transient meaning' (Mawson 2016: 5) that would be all that were possible without God.

---

[17] An additional, less influential rationale is that, with God, moral actions would be more important, apart from considerations of just responses to wrongdoing (Swinburne 2009, 2016: 154–8). For criticism of this position, see Section 6.3. Another argument, not yet fully developed, is that 'if you like mattering to others, mattering to a maximally excellent being would be maximally excellent' (Taliaferro 2016: 144; for additional hints, see Mawson 2013: 1143, and Metz 2013a: 122).

There are still other arguments in the literature that readers might consult, which are not squarely about the value of life's meaning. They are part of what is often called the 'pro-theist' position that a world with God would be better than (not necessarily in respect of life's meaning), or otherwise to be preferred relative to, a world without God. For a useful overview of pro-theist positions and their converse, anti-theist ones, see Kraay (2018a), and for the latest contributions to the debate between them, see the essays in Kraay (2018b).

[18] One might think that if a meaning is permanent, then there is more of it. That is probably true, but is not obviously so, for one could hold the view, say, that fleetingness would render a meaningful condition rare and for that reason more valuable than one that is eternal.

Even those who have advanced arguments for extreme forms of supernaturalism seem to hedge on occasion, speaking of an 'ultimate' meaning being possible only with God and a soul (Craig 2013; Cottingham 2016b: 135–6), which suggests that a less than ultimate meaning would be available without these spiritual conditions.[19] Similarly, one of them has spoken of a 'limited' or 'finite' sort of meaning being available on earth, contrasted with an 'unlimited' or 'infinite' one that logically depends on God (Nozick 1981: 618, 619; cf. Mawson 2016: 145; Swinburne 2016: 154).

The field has yet to distinguish carefully between the various senses of the 'great' sort of meaning that would purportedly be impossible in a purely physical world but that could come with a spiritual dimension. Above there were quantitative ('more', 'enough', 'infinite'), qualitative ('deep') and temporal ('permanent', with mention of 'lasting' in Moser 2016: 181–4) concepts. In addition, there might be more senses available – for example, how are we to understand what an 'unlimited' meaning connotes? It will be important to specify which senses of 'great' there are and how they matter relative to each other, if our understanding and hence evaluation of moderate supernaturalism is going to become particularly thorough.

However, the rest of this Section does not address this abstract, conceptual matter. Instead, it considers arguments for a moderate supernaturalism of some kind or other in respect of meaning in life,[20] where talk of a 'great' meaning admits of a variety of interpretations, for now. It is not particularly easy to advance an argument for moderate supernaturalism; this Section presents reason to believe that the most prominent rationales that have been put forward in support of it either provide no defence of supernaturalism at all relative to naturalism or collapse into the extreme form of supernaturalism.

5.2 An Afterlife Redux

One sort of argument for moderate supernaturalism appeals to the significance of an afterlife. Without a life after this bodily one on earth, many victims could not receive compensatory justice for their suffering and especially deaths, and retributive justice would also often enough fail to be done to their wrongdoers,

---

[19] And yet Craig in the same breath says that human mortality would render everything about our lives 'utterly meaningless' (2013: 160; see also Craig 2009b: 184).

[20] When it comes to the meaning of life, it is plausible to suggest that the human race would have at least somewhat more meaning if it had not been the product of chance and instead had sprung from an ideal person, been imparted with life as a gift or come into a world suffused with love (Seachris 2013: 14; Cottingham 2016b: 131; Mawson 2016: 64–6; Swinburne 2016: 154). Likewise, the human race as a whole would plausibly have more meaning if it helped God to defeat evil in the universe (Quinn 2000: 64–5; Mawson 2016: 57–64). These considerations about the significance of humanity should be weighed up against those addressed in Section 6.3.

making life much less meaningful than it could have been. Craig has again been influential in making the point that an atheist world cannot give people what they deserve:

> In the absence of moral accountability, our choices become trivialized because they make no ultimate contribution to either the betterment of the universe or to the moral good in general because everyone ends up the same. Death is the great leveler. (Craig 2009a: 38; see also Quinn 2000: 64; Craig 2009a: 31, 2009b: 183–4; Haught 2013: 178; Mawson 2013: 1141–2; Swinburne 2016: 157–9)

The phrasing suggests that one could make some moral contribution as a mortal being, but not an 'ultimate' one, which would presumably confer a greater meaning on life.

Apart from considerations of justice, entering Heaven would arguably confer great meaning on life for being a full realization of the life begun here, an 'eventual fulfillment of the human potential' (John Hick quoted in Haught 2013: 178). Perhaps one thereby reunites with friends and family, reconciles with enemies, achieves goals or receives reward for a life well lived, which would be much more meaningful than what is available to many of us in a purely physical world (Cottingham 2016b: 134–5; Moser 2016: 180–4; Swinburne 2016: 160–1).

There are two problems with these rationales, as they stand. The first is that, for all that has been said so far, it is conceivable that a purely physical world could do the important job for which a spiritual one is being deemed essential. Consider that any compensatory or retributively just response proportionate to what was done on earth could in principle take a physical form. Although justice is not, for all we can tell, perfectly done in this world if it is a purely physical one, it could be done in some other physical world, say, via an impersonal, karmic force that could track, amongst other things, brain states (Metz 2013a: 83, 108–9, 125, n. 2, 238–9; Kahane 2018). Similarly, it appears that any response that completes what was begun on earth could take a physical form. Again, reunion, reconciliation, achievement and reward all could be fully realized in an embodied state with a transfer of consciousness – and perhaps they *must* in order to be properly connected with what was begun in such a state. In principle, supernaturalism appears to gain no advantage relative to naturalism (granting that human beings in this world appear unable to bring about the relevant states of affairs on our own).

A tempting reply is: 'Only a religion with a creator God offers the possibility of compensation for the badness of my wasting my life' (Swinburne 2016: 157; see also Cottingham 2003: 64–73; Craig 2009b: 181). However, it is difficult to see why that is the case. Not only does one not need to have been *created* by a perfect, spiritual person in order for a being who is omnipotent to enable me to reach my full potential, one does not need *a spiritual person* at all. To be sure, our natural world does not appear to offer the possibility of compensation for everyone; however, another natural world, configured differently from this one, could do so.

A more promising reply to make to this point is instead to suggest that the relevant sort of justice, reunion, achievement and reward essentially involve God. Punishing wrongdoers means separating them from God, enjoying union of the most important sort would mean communing with God and so on. In short, the beatific vision should probably figure centrally (see Quinn 2000: 59; Mawson 2013: 1143, 2016: 155, 178; Swinburne 2016: 159–62).

Although deeming God to be essential to the content of the relevant afterlife would plausibly explain why we must have a spiritual nature, a second problem remains, namely, about why that nature must be immortal. Immortality does not seem essential to effect justice or to complete a life begun on earth. Finite deeds warrant finite responses, when it comes to justice. Sacrifices made in this world to help others do not deserve eternal bliss in another world, and not even torture and murder seem to warrant an infinite amount of torment. Furthermore, careers, relationships and hobbies do not appear to demand a never-ending life in which to realize them fully. Why would a few thousand more years not suffice? Granting, at this stage of the dialectic, that one needs to be in the presence of God in order for an afterlife to matter greatly, it does not follow that one must be in His presence forever.

Let us suppose, though, that an everlasting life with God would not constitute merely a greater meaning, but the greatest one. In that case, we would have a rationale for God and a soul as essential for a certain type of meaning unavailable in an atheist world. However, the concern now is that this rationale collapses into the extreme form of supernaturalism.[21] The logic of this rationale threatens to render it unable to capture the essential intuition, accepted by the moderate supernaturalist, that a meaningful life without God is possible. If an eternal afterlife spent with God would enhance meaning in our lives, it would do so to such a huge extent as to make it unreasonable to judge an eighty-year life as capable of being meaningful. Compare the degree of meaning in an immortal life in Heaven with the degree available to a mortal life. It would be infinitely larger. And if such a life would be infinitely more meaningful than a mortal one, then the grounds for claiming that a mortal life could be meaningful on balance fall away. It would be like saying that a house can be big, even if it would be bigger were it to grow to be the size of a billion billion billion suns.

---

[21] The next two paragraphs borrow from Metz (2018: 187–8).

Mawson, a moderate supernaturalist quoted earlier in this Element as accepting that Gandhi's life would be meaningful in a world without God or a soul, comes close to acknowledging the point at times. For example, Mawson remarks:

> [E]ven the meaning that can be enjoyed in a lifespan of several millennia will ultimately amount to a small dollop when compared with that enjoyed everlastingly *post-mortem*. And again, given that the afterlife is potentially infinite, so any finite dollop will diminish in relative size, tending to nothing over time. (2016: 144; see also 13, 154)

This concern is serious, since the intuition that Mawson and others these days are seeking to capture is that a meaningful life on balance is possible in an atheist world, just not of a sort that is particularly or most desirable. To be sure, by this position, Gandhi's life would not be a 'flat zero', but it would, compared to infinity, come about as close to zero as is mathematically possible for a non-zero number, and that arguably fails to capture the judgement that Gandhi's life was meaningful on balance absent God and a soul. Just as we would not describe someone's life as 'happy' if it had only a smidge of happiness compared to what is frequently on offer, so we cannot plausibly describe someone's mortal life as 'meaningful' if it has only a small dollop of meaning compared to infinity.

The moderate supernaturalist needs to explain how we can avoid thinking that the value of an infinite afterlife would ridiculously outweigh that of a finite lifespan, reducing it to next to nothing by comparison, thereby leaving us unable to capture the intuition that a finite lifespan could ever count as meaningful on balance.[22] She cannot suggest that judgements of whether someone's life is meaningful are not comparative, for at the core of her view is precisely a comparative judgement, viz., that a spiritual dimension would alone make possible a greater, if not the greatest, sort of meaning in life. So, there needs to be reflection on how to make proper judgements of when a person's life counts as a meaningful one, and in particular of how they are affected by comparisons with other, actual and merely potential lives.

5.3 Being Part of God's Life

Another rationale that has been advanced explicitly in support of moderate supernaturalism is that our lives could enjoy a greater meaning only if we

---

[22] For the way Mawson addresses this concern, see Mawson (2018: 202–3). Matthew Hammerton has suggested in conversation that a life might be infinitely long in duration and continue to accrue meaning over time, but ever increasingly to a lesser degree, so that it never achieves whichever amount of meaning would dwarf the meaning available to a finite life. It is an interesting move, but one then wonders whether this eternal life would, at a certain stage, be comparable to one in a permanent coma, which may be presumed to have some, small amount of meaning (say, in respect of loved ones), but not enough to make it worth continuing to live.

became part of God's life. Although some understand that concept essentially, such that 'without us God would not be God' (Smith 2000: 256), the more frequent view is that meaning would come from sharing a life with Him, where He could have existed without us.

Sharing a life with God, here, does not mean enjoying an afterlife in His presence, the sort of rationale from the previous Sub-Section. Instead, the thought is that, by living a certain way while on earth, our lives can have a 'cosmic significance ... instead of a significance very limited in time and space' (Swinburne 2016: 154). Without God, our lives could be meaningful in only 'a local and temporary sense' (Cottingham 2016b: 136).

For example, if we were to help realize God's plan for the universe while on earth, then our actions would arguably have a much greater importance by virtue of their role in a benevolent project that is as large and long-lasting as one can get for covering 'the whole universe and all its inhabitants' (Swinburne 2016: 154, and see also 156–8; Quinn 2000: 58–65). In partnering with God to fight evil, our lives would acquire a much greater meaning because of the massive spatio-temporal scope of the endeavour in this world.

For another example, consider the eternal effect of so acting on another world, specifically, on God's mind. In particular, consider God forever fondly remembering what one did to help to realize His purpose, something eloquently emphasized by John Cottingham:

> The sense that our acts are eternally subject to divine evaluation ... seems deeply to enhance their significance [as] a source of joy to a being of supreme wisdom and love. This amplifies and as it were confirms the meaningfulness that they already had on earth, and protects them against the erosions of time and contingency, shielding them against the backdrop of impermanence against which nothing in the long term matters very much. (2016b: 135; see also 131–4, as well as Hartshorne 1984, and Swinburne 2016: 154)

In addition to speaking here of a 'deep' enhancement of significance, Cottingham invokes temporal considerations, remarking that if 'our acts are eternally subject to divine evaluation ... our contribution ultimately and eternally matters' (Cottingham 2016b: 135).

The kinds of objections made to the previous rationale for moderate super-naturalism prima facie apply to this one.[23] That is, either a physical world is sufficient to realize the putatively great meaning or, if it is not, then the spiritual

---

[23] For an additional objection, there is the interesting suggestion that it is only in an atheist world that our lives could be cosmically significant, since in a theist one we would be insignificant compared to God (Kahane 2014).

greatness would be 'too big' to capture the intuition that a purely physical life could be meaningful.

First off, envision generations of mortal humans (or perhaps post- or trans-humans) recounting tales of a person's deeds successively without end in an infinitely expanding universe, where their remembrance inspires many others to do their best in an intergalactic exchange of cultures. This physicalist form of remembrance appears sufficient to confer the relevant sort of meaning, with no spiritual realm being necessary. Why think it must be God with the plan and who remembers forever one's contribution to its fulfilment? Might it be because only He could remember literally everyone who has ever existed all at the same time (Hartshorne 1984)?

Second, if it were indeed only God who could ground a plan of the requisite infinite scope, then it would not be clear that the supernaturalism could coherently remain moderate as opposed to extreme. Arguably the greatness of an act that has a 'cosmic significance' or that 'eternally matters' must dwarf any meaning lacking this feature, making it difficult to explain how a merely earthly life could, by comparison, be meaningful, which the moderate supernaturalist accepts is possible.

5.4 Satisfaction of Deep Desires

A different sort of argument for moderate supernaturalism appeals to a ranking of what human beings characteristically want. By this argument, the moderate supernaturalist will grant that a naturalist sort of meaning could satisfy some of our 'surface desires' (Seachris 2013: 20, n. 47), or at best our mid-level needs, longings and wishes. However, he will maintain that only a supernatural meaning could satisfy 'profound desires anchored in the core of our being' (Seachris 2013: 20, n. 47), 'fundamental human aspirations' (Cottingham 2016b: 136) or 'the voracious human hunger for meaning' (Haught 2013: 176; see also Seachris 2011: 154, 2013: 14; Goetz 2012: 44, 47; Cottingham 2016b: 127).

In particular, some suggest that: 'If the universe is all there is, and if it is therefore devoid of purpose, then one must conclude that nature is *not enough* to fill our restless human hearts with the meaning we long for' (Haught 2013: 176). And others naturally maintain that eternal happiness, consisting of pleasure, is what we all most crave (see especially Goetz 2012: 44, 47).

The problem with this reasoning is that it just does not seem true to say that human beings qua human beings desire a world with a purposive God or a blissful soul. In particular, many in the South and East Asian traditions simply do not hanker for the existence of God or a soul as construed in this Element. Literally billions of adherents to Hinduism and Confucianism, for example, have desires radically different from believers in Judaism, Christianity and Islam. If so, then a spiritual realm is not necessary for them to have a greater sort of meaning, by the logic of the present argument. Indeed, if there is in fact no spiritual dimension, and if our desires are malleable, then one would be best off letting go of desires for perfection that cannot be fulfilled (on which see Trisel 2002).

Advocates of the desire-based argument for moderate supernaturalism need to reflect more on how to make the case that there is something about human nature as such that tends towards desires for theistic spiritual conditions. They must accept that many human beings do not in fact desire the existence of God or a soul, and it would be implausible to suggest that this is merely because these human beings have lacked these concepts. How, then, might moderate supernaturalists reasonably contend that there is something inherent to human nature about the desire for theism? Perhaps they would suggest that even if people do not all desire theism to be true, it is essential for satisfying other desires that they do all have. Yet, Hindus – many of whom proclaim to want not to be a separate self and instead to want to unite properly with an unconscious force that grounds the universe – loom especially large.

5.5 An Objection to Arguments for Moderate Supernaturalism en Masse

To conclude this Section, consider a problem facing all three of the aforementioned rationales for a moderate supernaturalism. It is that the opportunity for greater meaning with a spiritual dimension would bring in its wake a corresponding opportunity for greater 'anti-matter' (Metz 2013a: 63–4, 71–2, 234–5) or 'anti-meaning' (Campbell and Nyholm 2015), roughly, conditions that would reduce meaning in life. If the prospective gains with God or a soul would be much greater, then so would the prospective losses, and the field has yet to reflect carefully on which world, theist or atheist, would be better in respect of life's meaning.

By 'anti-matter' and related terms is meant conditions that are not merely the lack of meaning, that is, the absence of a positive, but that detract from the amount of meaning in a life, the presence of a negative. Consider the difference between oversleeping by an hour and using that hour to torture an innocent stranger for the fun of it. There would be an absence of meaning in both, but plausibly a reduction of meaning in one's life in the latter, because of the substantive disvalue.

Now, the present objection to the three arguments for moderate supernaturalism addressed in this Section is that they, by parity of reasoning, entail that with the chance at great meaning would come the comparable chance at great anti-meaning. Specifically, if moral accountability requires the prospect of eternal life in a Heaven, it also requires the prospect of eternal life in a Hell. If one's good deeds and God's being pleased about them would produce a greater significance for one's existence than would be possible in a world without Him, then one's bad deeds and His displeasure at them would reduce the significance of one's life to a correspondingly greater degree. And if a world with God and a soul are what alone could realize one's deepest desires, e.g., to fulfil a purpose for the universe so as to merit great esteem, then the same world could alone offer the possibility of one's living in such a way that one fails to fulfil that purpose, which would merit great shame.

The point of the present argument is not that the chances of a life empty of meaning would increase in a world with a spiritual dimension; it is rather that the chances of a life full of anti-matter would increase with it, supposing, for the sake of argument, that those of a meaningful life would increase with it. If this latter claim is true, do the expected value and expected disvalue in respect of meaning 'cancel out', so that there is no rational ground to favour a theist world relative to an atheist one, or vice versa? Or, would the rational thing, so far as life's meaning is concerned, be to play it safe and prefer to avoid any chance at Hell, hence favouring an atheist world? Or would one have such ample opportunity to avoid Hell in a theist world that it would be rational to prefer it, despite the grave disvalue possible in respect of meaning in life? Is there a rationale for moderate supernaturalism that is not vulnerable to this parity objection and that could avoid these complications?

6 Extreme Naturalism

The previous Section on naturalism was labelled 'moderate', since the arguments in it supported merely the conclusions that a spiritual realm is not necessary for life's meaning and that a physical one would be sufficient for that. These points are consistent with a kind of supernaturalism according to which God or a soul could alone confer a great meaning on life, even if they are not essential for meaning as such. The present Section considers an 'extreme naturalism', one that rejects even such a moderate supernaturalism. The conclusions drawn here are that it would be better in respect of at least meaning in life if there were no God or a soul and there existed only a physical world.

The Section begins by noting the twentieth-century origins of extreme naturalism (6.1), but uses more space to address newer positions that are salient in the twenty-first century. After addressing arguments for thinking that more meaning in life could obtain without a soul (6.2), the Section considers those for thinking that more meaning could obtain without God (6.3).

6.1 The Rise of Extreme Naturalism

Extreme naturalism initially grew out of existentialist and subjectivist philosophies that were popular in the twentieth century. For example, Jean-Paul Sartre was perhaps the first to voice adherence to an extreme form of naturalism, at least in the context of literature explicitly devoted to life's meaning.[24] For him, God is not merely unnecessary for life to have meaning, but would reduce it, for if God existed and had created us for a purpose, then our lives would be degraded for being akin to the status of a knife or some other artefact. In his famous essay 'Existentialism Is a Humanism', Sartre said this of his view that the meaning of a person's life is a function of whichever choices she has made: '[T]his theory alone is compatible with the dignity of man, it is the only one which does not make man into an object' (1956: 302; see also Singer 1996: 29; Baier 2000: 104; Salles 2010). If an individual's purpose has not been self-fashioned, but has rather been assigned to her, then she is being treated like a thing, which, as a source of shame as opposed to pride, reduces the meaning in her life.

There is a concern about a tension in this position, in which it appears that degradation is an objective disvalue for the putatively subjectivist Sartre. Beyond that point, many have argued that being assigned a purpose by God need not be degrading or otherwise meaning-reducing, at least on balance (for the longer discussions, see Walker 1989; Cottingham 2005: 37–57; Metz 2013a: 99–104, 2013c; Mawson 2016: 110–33).

Another early rationale for extreme naturalism targeted not God, but a soul. Bernard Williams is well known amongst Anglo-American philosophers for having advanced the view that the ultimate reasons for a person to act are grounded on that person's 'categorical desires', roughly, what she desires for its own sake and not for the sake of satisfying some further desire. According to Williams, if we had a soul and hence were immortal, our lives would be meaningless roughly because we would at some point fulfil our categorical desires and be left bored with nothing else to do (1973; for a recent proponent, see Belshaw 2005: 82–91).

The responses to Williams' reasoning are legion. Most have taken the form of contending that an eternal life need not get boring (for just a few of the many

---

[24] Karl Marx and Friedrich Nietzsche held that belief in God reduced meaning in a life (even if they did not use that language), but it is not as clear that they thought that God's existence would do so.

discussions, see Fischer 1994; Wisnewski 2005; Chappell 2009; Bortolotti and Nagasawa 2009). However, it is also worth questioning the premise that boredom is necessarily incompatible with meaning in life. What if, say, one voluntarily underwent boredom in order to prevent others from being bored? Might that choice confer some meaning on one's life?

As has been spelled out, the initial arguments for extreme naturalism sprang from the ideas that the value of meaning in a person's life must be created by her choices or that reasons of meaning are relative to a person's desires. However, considerations of degradation and boredom need not be a function of subjectivism about values or reasons. And the more recent arguments for extreme naturalism, considered in the rest of this Section, are usually premised on an objective approach, which has been noticeably on the rise over the past thirty years or so.[25]

6.2 Reasons to Reject a Soul

Some arguments advanced against having a soul or otherwise being immortal appear, upon reflection, to be best construed as objections to having a belief in it.[26] Consider, for instance, the claim that if one would live forever, then one would not prioritize or be motivated to do very much, in the expectation of another tomorrow in which to get everything done (James 2009; May 2009: 45–7, 60–72; Scheffler 2013: 99–101). Strictly speaking, the logic of this argument applies to belief in a soul, not actually having one. If one were in fact immortal but did not think one were, then one would prioritize and be properly motivated, and, conversely, if one were in fact mortal but did not think one were, then one would not (to the extent the argument succeeds).

The same concern applies, at least to some degree, to the suggestion that if we were immortal, our lives could not display an important sort of virtue (Nussbaum 1989: 338–9; Wielenberg 2005: 91–2). If we cannot die, then we cannot risk our lives for the sake of others, and if others cannot die, then we can cannot save anyone else's life. It seems that the meaningfulness of being a doctor, lifeguard, firefighter or the like depends on our not having a soul and instead having only this earthly, mortal life. Now, although it is true that life and death matters would not be at stake, much virtue could be displayed, if an agent incorrectly believed that people were mortal. Imagine that when a fireman runs into a burning building to rescue children trapped inside, he thinks that he is putting his life at risk to rescue their lives that are at risk. In fact, though, if his

---

[25] For the argument that God's existence would necessarily occlude a subjective sort of meaning, see Mawson (2016: 110–33).

[26] Some ideas and phrasings in the next two paragraphs have been culled from Metz (2017a: 364–6).

body or the children's bodies were to die, their mental states would remain contained within souls that survive. Such a fireman, despite being immortal, would, because of his motivation, plausibly exhibit the virtues of courage and beneficence (at least to a noteworthy extent).

It is of course worth thinking more about these arguments, upon positing knowledge on the part of the agents involved. If one did know that one is immortal, would one then be motivated to make something of one's life or be able to display real courage? However, the rest of this Section instead addresses arguments against immortality the logic of which do not depend so much on a person's propositional attitudes about the length of her life.

One such argument is that living forever would unavoidably become repetitive, which would undercut the prospect of meaning in it (Scarre 2007: 54–5; May 2009: 46–7, 64–5; Smuts 2011: 142–4; cf. Blumenfeld 2009). Suppose the previous concerns about being immortal were resolved. That is, knowing that one is immortal, imagine that one could stave off boredom, make much of one's time and display important virtues. Even so, there appear to be only a finite number of actions that one could perform in an infinite amount of time, in which case one must end up doing the same things. And doing the same things would be incompatible with the growth, progress or at least variety that many associate with a life's being meaningful. After all, classic images of meaninglessness include Sisyphus rolling a rock up a hill for eternity (famously discussed in Camus 1955) and factory workers conforming to the dictates of an assembly line.

Even those who enjoyed doing much good for others would be robbed of real meaning if these activities were to repeat. Consider the movie *Groundhog Day*, in which the main character, upon having become a better person who is glad to be kind to others, still repeats the same twenty-four hours over and over again. Happily engaging in repetitive activities, and ones that involve helping others, would surely be better than hating activities that do no good for anyone, but, even so, the repetition in itself would, for many of us, seriously detract from the meaning they might have had.

The concern about repetition in an immortal life is underdeveloped in the literature. Must, indeed, much of an immortal life repeat itself? Might there be something about having a soul, perhaps one contemplating an infinite being, that would enable a person to avoid repeating the same things over the course of an eternity? If repetition is unavoidable, might meaning reside in the ability to display certain attitudes in the face of an eternal recurrence of the same (suggested by Nietzsche)? Or might substantial enough meaning be available from the parts of one's life considered in themselves, even if they repeated some millions or billions of years down the road?

Another argument against having a soul or otherwise living forever also invokes considerations about the pattern of the life as a whole. Some maintain that essential to a particularly meaningful life is some kind of narrative, where there could not be a narrative to an eternal life (Scarre 2007: 58–60). At the core of a narrative is a beginning, a middle and an end, and the suggestion is that a life that never ends would be incapable of forming a narrative. An existence without a life-story could be happy or moral, so the argument goes, but would be missing meaning in it, or at least one key sort. Relatedly, there has been the suggestion that our agency would not feature prominently in an immortal life; time and contingencies would instead be what principally shape it (Wollheim 1984: 265–7; Cholbi 2015).

In reply, thoughtful work has been done on what kinds of narratives there could be insofar as they bear on life's meaning, with efforts to demonstrate that an eternal life could still have an end, or at least constitute a narrative, in an important sense. One suggestion is that a collection of short stories that grow out of each other could count as a relevant sort of narrative on which to model a meaningful immortality (Fischer 2005). Another idea – deeming life to be ideally more akin to a novel – is that one sort of a life's ending that matters is a function of what its content is and how that relates to what came before, neither of which need involve temporal finality (Seachris 2011, 2016). Whereas the first suggestion appears to involve no sense of closure to a life-story, the second one does, imagining, say, (eternal) flourishing consequent to having undertaken some labour or to having distanced oneself from one's sinful nature. And advocates of either approach would naturally contend that agency would be central to imparting the relevant sort of immortal narrative.

6.3 Reasons to Reject God

Sartre's concern about God unavoidably treating His creation 'as an object' continues to resonate amongst extreme naturalists, although there is now a different language and somewhat different concepts too, in what is sometimes called the 'anti-theist' literature.[27] Much of the recent discussion has been focused on talk of 'independence' (Kahane 2011, 2018; Lougheed 2017), which signifies a cluster of issues.

One issue is that there would unavoidably be costs to failing to help God to realize His plan for the universe, if not the threat of Hell or some kind of punishment, then at least the psychological costs of disobedience. A second is that we would never be alone in the world, as God would constantly be aware of our thoughts and be influencing the course of human life. A third is that God

---

[27] In contrast to the 'pro-theism' mentioned earlier in this Element.

would have a status much higher than ours, e.g., He would deserve an attitude of worship, and in our actions we would have to 'bend the knee' to His will. An interesting, fourth variant is that in order to prevent an unfair condition in which some are more able to achieve God's purpose than others, God would have to tailor-make each of us to achieve a single purpose, which would be restrictive, manipulative or degrading of a freedom to find meaning from a variety of sources (Salles 2010). Although these arguments are usually advanced in respect of meaning in life, at least some of them (most clearly the one concerning status) prima facie apply to the meaning of life too.

Most of these concerns remain, even if one supposes, for the sake of argument, that God would not penalize us for disobedience and that we would be well off if we were to obey Him. The issues are instead about how God would treat us and how we would have to treat God. They are in the main ultimately about the objective badness, or anti-matter, of the indignity of servility and conformity.

Philosophers have made a variety of replies to these kinds of concerns. First, some deny that there would be servility or dependence of objectionable sorts. After all, meaning would surely not come from freely deciding to become a serial killer, while God would plausibly allow human persons enough of the intuitively important sorts of freedom (e.g. Penner 2015: 334–7, 2017; Cottingham 2016b: 125–7). Second, others contend that if a lack of complete independence in a world with God were objectionable, the same lack of complete independence would obtain in a world without God, providing no reason to favour an atheist world (Penner 2017). Third, still others maintain that even if it were true that with God would uniquely come objectionable sorts of dependence, on balance our lives would enjoy a net gain in meaningfulness (e.g. Kraay and Dragos 2013).

Along with (or part of) a lack of independence has been a concern regarding a lack of privacy that would be unavoidable if God existed (Kahane 2011, 2018; Lougheed 2017). God's being all-good and hence a perfect moral judge means that He would be apprised of all our mental states. God's being all-knowing likewise appears sufficient for Him to know everything about us. Although friendship and love, at their most meaningful, do involve a revelation to another person of who one is deep down, this disclosure is characteristically voluntary. In the case of God, however, He would be acquainted with our complete selves without our consent, where such intrusion removes meaning that one could have had (and perhaps is even anti-meaningful).

In reply, some argue that the absence of privacy would not matter since God would be sure to love us and hence care for our deepest ailments (Penner 2015: 336–7). Others reply, interestingly, that if it were indeed the case that a lack of privacy would be incompatible with treating us beneficently or otherwise morally appropriately, then God would ensure that He lacks complete knowledge of our mental states (Tooley 2018). Such a lack would be compatible with His being properly described as 'omniscient', since that is plausibly understood as knowledge up to the point at which it is morally permissible to have.

A third prominent argument for thinking that more meaning would come from an atheist world[28] turns on the impossibility of making certain kinds of moral sacrifice in a world with God (Wielenberg 2005: 91–4; Hubin 2009; Maitzen 2009; Sinnott-Armstrong 2009: 114). In at least one atheist world, people could face the prospect of undeserved harm, where substantial meaning in life intuitively would come from an agent making a sacrifice so that others do not suffer that. It would, for instance, confer some meaning on one's life to suffer some pain in order to prevent an innocent child from being burned alive. However, by a standard conception of God, He would always compensate any undeserved harm suffered while on earth.[29] That means that a mother who undergoes pain in order to prevent her son from experiencing intense suffering makes no real sacrifice, since God will make it up to her. It also means that anything done to help the boy did no real good, since God would have made it up to the child were he to suffer. In a world with God, then, a central source of meaning from moral sacrifice is absent since that depends on the ability to undergo a net loss on the part of both the agent and the patient.

In reply, some have asserted that undergoing hardship for the sake of others in the here and now counts as a 'self-sacrifice', even if it is compensated in an afterlife (Goetz 2012: 70), but a bit more needs to be said in order to show that this sort of self-sacrifice would confer meaning. On this score, another maintains, as was suggested earlier in this Element (6.2), that 'altruism has to do with the agent's motivations for action' (Craig 2009b: 174), regardless of whether the agent suffers a net harm or the patient is prevented from suffering one. However, even if the virtue of altruism (or beneficence, etc.) were exhausted by motivational states, or at least were not a function of objective matters of fact about undeserved harm, it is plausible that virtue would not, in that case, exhaust the meaningfulness of altruism. The significance of the helping action does seem to depend to some extent on whether an agent pays a real cost, or at least on whether a patient is given a real benefit.

---

[28] A fourth argument for extreme naturalism, still nascent, is that our understanding of the basic nature of reality would be impaired if God existed (Kahane 2011: 682; Maitzen 2018; cf. Swinburne 2016: 154).

[29] Doing so would not appear to require us to have a soul, and hence this argument is not placed in Sub-Section 6.2.

Perhaps a more promising line would be to marshal evidence that being a source of a desirable state of affairs can be meaning-conferring, even if the desirable state of affairs would have obtained anyway.[30] Consider that one does not merely want one's son to be reared with love, but one also wants to be the one who rears him with love. This desire remains even knowing that others would have reared him with love in one's absence, so that one's actions would not be increasing the final value of the state of the universe relative to what it would have had without them. Even if a stepmother would have appeared on the scene and produced the same effects on one's son, it is intuitive to think that some meaning accrues to one's life for an agent-relative consideration, namely, for in fact having been the one to have produced these effects. What goes for a stepmother analogously applies to the God-father; even if He would have stepped in to compensate a boy in full for pain he had unjustly suffered, some meaning would plausibly accrue if one of us had prevented the pain to that child in the first place. Meaning can come from making others in the world better off, even if one does not make them better off than they would have been without one.

This reasoning, if sound, would explain why it is not necessary to prevent a moral patient from suffering a net harm in order for altruism to be meaningful. However, it leaves untouched the suggestion that meaning also comes from a moral agent undergoing a net harm in the course of being altruistic.

On this score, it is open to the supernaturalist to bite the bullet and to deny that the meaningfulness of helping others depends on one's being harmed without compensation, even if it does depend on making some kind of effort. Suppose one can rescue either two people without one undergoing a net harm, or a single person in the course of bringing a net harm to oneself. It is reasonable to suggest that more meaning would accrue in the former case, which is well explained by the irrelevance of agent sacrifice for altruist meaning.

Indeed, the supernaturalist could make a deft dialectical move by pointing out that, by the dominant naturalist approach to meaning, one must be subjectively attracted to what one is doing for it to arise (4.1). If an agent is supposed to like or enjoy his worthwhile activities, then incurring a net harm such as pain in the course of preventing another's suffering is probably not meaning-conferring, by the naturalist's own, widely held view.

Finally, even if the naturalist were correct that moral self-sacrifice would confer no meaning in a world with God, the supernaturalist can contend that God would make other facets of a moral life more important on balance

---

[30] The rest of this paragraph borrows from Metz (2017b: 16–17), which includes additional examples.

(Swinburne 2009, 2016: 154–6). For instance, if we mistreated other human beings in a theist world we would not merely wrong them, but also the one responsible for their creation and in whose image they were made. This reply, of arguing that, all things considered, God would add more meaning than He would subtract in respect of morality, could be made, *mutatis mutandis*, to the entire disagreement between moderate supernaturalists and extreme naturalists, as the concluding Section discusses.

7 Concluding Remarks: Further Reflection on God and Soul

As the reader might have noticed from the dates of the works cited in the previous two Sections, the debates between moderate supernaturalists and extreme naturalists are fresh indeed. A large majority of works explicitly arguing that a spiritual dimension would either add to or instead subtract from life's meaning (as opposed to be either necessary for it or not) have appeared only in about the past dozen years. Many issues remain under-theorized, as this Element has sought to highlight in previous Sections, making firm conclusions difficult at this stage. The Element concludes by suggesting some additional, and more overarching, ways by which to take the contemporary debates forward.

As mentioned at the end of the previous Section, a promising way to respond to the claim that God or a soul would reduce life's meaning compared to a world without them is to contend that, even if this were true in one respect, redeeming features of a spiritual dimension exist that would, on balance, greatly enhance life's meaning. For instance, one might suggest that, although God's existence might impair our independence and hence subtract from life's meaning to some degree, an atheist world would entail that the wicked go unpunished and more generally that we cannot be part of God's plan for good to triumph over evil, which would be even less meaningful by comparison.

Now, the same strategy may of course be employed by the extreme naturalist: even if it were true that God or a soul would in some ways enhance life's meaning compared to a world without them, perhaps there would be undercutting features of a spiritual dimension that, on balance, would reduce it. For example, although communing with God forever in Heaven might confer more meaning of a sort than would be available in an atheist world, that life could not avoid becoming repetitive, which would arguably ruin the narrative and make life not worth continuing.

In order to make progress here, a good first step would be to obtain clarity on what conceptually can make a source of life's meaning great or not. Earlier

in this Element, recall, there were quantitative, qualitative and temporal interpretations of greatness, and the possibility of still others (5.1). Are these various
distinctions at bottom a function of one, say, the quantitative? That is, do we
want a deep or lasting meaning ultimately merely because it would confer more
meaning on life than a shallow or transient one? Or, in contrast, would one of
these kinds of meaning ground a reason for action or judgement that is inde-
pendent of the amount of meaning involved? If the former, would an eternal
meaning necessarily produce an infinite amount of it? If the latter, how are we
to balance considerations of, say, quantity and quality when settling our pre-
ferences and more generally living our lives?

Another project worth undertaking would be to distinguish carefully between
conditions that would prevent the good of meaning in life and those that would
consist of anti-matter and so would be a bad that takes meaning away from
a person's life. For example, presumably the concerns about motivation and
certain virtues not being possible if we have a soul are best understood as saying
that a spiritual dimension would prevent meaning that could have otherwise
come, not that it would be anti-meaningful. In contrast, the worry that God
would necessarily entail servility on our part is straightforwardly construed as
a substantive reduction of meaning in our lives, not merely the prevention of
some other positive source of meaning.

Sometimes, though, it is hard to tell whether a condition taken to make us
worse off in respect of meaning consists of the prevention of a positive or the
constitution of a negative. Consider, say, the absence of privacy that might
come with God's existence, or the presence of repetition that a soul might
unavoidably bring in its wake. Would these conditions mean less meaning in
a spiritual world relative to a purely physical one because they would prevent
the positives of a relationship with voluntary disclosure or a life with
a developmental narrative, or, in contrast, because they are final disvalues?

Furthermore, recall the question of whether a source of meaning and a
parallel source of anti-meaning necessarily 'cancel out' or not, when it comes
to ascertaining which world would be most desirable in respect of meaning
(5.5). For instance, if Heaven would be a much greater source of meaning than
what could be on offer in an atheist world, then presumably Hell would be
a comparably greater source of anti-meaning than what could be on offer in it.
If so, would there be no net gain for a theist world relative to an atheist one, or
are differential chances of facing these outcomes in a theist world relevant?
If they are, then how is one to weigh them up? Does one calculate the expected
value, or does one instead use a more conservative decision rule, such as
preferring a world in which the worst-off result would not go below a certain
threshold?

Finally, for now, it is worth starting to make tentative comparative judgements of, say, amounts of meaning, and looking for patterns. To see what could be involved here, consider an analogy with degrees of moral wrongness. Some acts are more wrong, that is, morally worse, than others. Consequentialists can account for degrees of wrongness in terms of amounts final dis/value that were not produced but that could have been. Kantian deontologists can do so in terms of the extent to which autonomy was reduced, or they might suggest that, all things being equal, internal interference, say, with the mind or the body, is more degrading than external interference, e.g., with a person's property. When it comes to life's meaning, it would be useful to posit similar structures when making judgements of how much of it is lost, or, conversely, gained. All the field really has at the moment are the consequentialist claim that the more final good one produces, the more meaningful one's life (e.g. Smuts 2013), and the suggestion that eternal life brings the prospect of infinite meaning (e.g. Mawson 2016). How else might one plausibly compare two conditions in respect of the amount of meaning they would add or instead subtract? Or how might one rank different types of meaning?

There is, as the field stands, virtually no literature addressing any of the questions posed here, the pertinence of which should be clear in the light of having read this Element. Although debates over whether God or a soul might be necessary for life's meaning as such can and should continue, they have already gone on for some centuries. Substantial disagreements about whether a spiritual dimension might instead contribute to, or conversely detract from, life's meaning are by comparison new, and may this Element prompt readers to take them forward in particular.[31]

---

[31] For useful comments on a prior draft of this Element, I thank anonymous referees for Cambridge University Press.

Bibliography

Affolter, Jacob. 2007. 'Human Nature As God's Purpose'. *Religious Studies* 43: 443–55.

Audi, Robert. 2005. 'Intrinsic Value and Meaningful Life'. *Philosophical Papers* 34: 331–55.

Ayer, Alfred Jules. 2000. 'The Claims of Philosophy'. Repr. in E. D. Klemke (ed.), *The Meaning of Life*, 2nd edn. New York: Oxford University Press, 219–33. First published in 1947.

Baier, Kurt. 2000. 'The Meaning of Life'. Repr. in E. D. Klemke (ed.), *The Meaning of Life*, 2nd edn. New York: Oxford University Press, 101–32. First published in 1957.

Baker, Lynne Rudder. 2017. 'Resurrecting Material Persons'. In Yujin Nagasawa and Benjamin Matheson (eds), *The Palgrave Handbook of the Afterlife*. London: Palgrave Macmillan, 315–30.

Belshaw, Christopher. 2005. *10 Good Questions about Life and Death*. Malden, MA: Blackwell.

Bennett-Hunter, Guy. 2014. *Ineffability and Religious Experience*. Oxford: Routledge.

Bennett-Hunter, Guy. 2016. 'Ineffability'. *Philosophia* 44: 1267–87.

Blessing, Kimberly. 2013. 'Atheism and the Meaningfulness of Life'. In Stephen Bullivant and Michael Ruse (eds), *The Oxford Handbook of Atheism*. Oxford: Oxford University Press, 104–18.

Blumenfeld, David. 2009. 'Living Life over Again'. *Philosophy and Phenomenological Research* 79: 357–86.

Bortolotti, Lisa and Nagasawa, Yujin. 2009. 'Immortality without Boredom'. *Ratio* 22: 261–77.

Brown, Delwin. 1971. 'Process Philosophy and the Question of Life's Meaning'. *Religious Studies* 7: 13–29.

Campbell, Stephen and Nyholm, Sven. 2015. 'Anti-Meaning and Why It Matters'. *Journal of the American Philosophical Association* 1: 694–711.

Camus, Albert. 1955. *The Myth of Sisyphus*, Justin O'Brian (trans.). Repr. London: H. Hamilton. First published in 1942.

Chappell, Timothy. 2009. 'Infinity Goes up on Trial: Must Immortality Be Meaningless?' *European Journal of Philosophy* 17: 30–44.

Cholbi, Michael. 2015. 'Immortality and the Exhaustibility of Value'. In Michael Cholbi (ed.), *Immortality and the Philosophy of Death*. Lanham, MD: Rowman and Littlefield, 221–36.

Cooper, David. 2003. *Meaning*. Durham: Acumen Publishing.

Cottingham, John. 2003. *On the Meaning of Life*. London: Routledge.

Cottingham, John. 2005. *The Spiritual Dimension: Religion, Philosophy and Human Value*. Cambridge: Cambridge University Press.

Cottingham, John. 2008. 'The Self, the Good Life and the Transcendent'. In Nafsika Athanassoulis and Samantha Vice (eds), *The Moral Life: Essays in Honour of John Cottingham*. New York: Palgrave Macmillan, 231–74.

Cottingham, John. 2016a. 'Theism and Meaning in Life'. *European Journal for Philosophy of Religion* 8: 47–58.

Cottingham, John. 2016b. 'Meaningfulness, Eternity, and Theism'. In Joshua Seachris and Stewart Goetz (eds), *God and Meaning*. New York: Bloomsbury Academic, 123–36.

Craig, William Lane. 2009a. 'The Kurtz/Craig Debate'. In Robert Garcia and Nathan King (eds), *Is Goodness without God Good Enough?* Lanham, MD: Rowman and Littlefield, 23–46.

Craig, William Lane. 2009b. 'This Most Gruesome of Guests'. In Robert Garcia and Nathan King (eds), *Is Goodness without God Good Enough?* Lanham, MD: Rowman and Littlefield, 167–88.

Craig, William Lane. 2013. 'The Absurdity of Life without God'. Repr. in Joshua Seachris (ed.), *Exploring the Meaning of Life: An Anthology and Guide*. Malden, MA: Wiley-Blackwell, 153–72. First published in 1994.

Davis, William. 1987. 'The Meaning of Life'. *Metaphilosophy* 18: 288–305.

Edwards, Paul. 1972. 'Why'. In Paul Edwards (ed.), *The Encyclopedia of Philosophy, Volumes 7–8*. New York: Macmillan Publishing Company, 296–302.

Ellis, Fiona. 2011. 'Desire, Infinity, and the Meaning of Life'. *Philosophy* 86: 483–502.

Fischer, John Martin. 1994. 'Why Immortality Is Not So Bad'. *International Journal of Philosophical Studies* 2: 257–70.

Fischer, John Martin. 2005. 'Free Will, Death, and Immortality: The Role of Narrative'. *Philosophical Papers* 34: 379–403.

Frankfurt, Harry. 1988. 'The Importance of What We Care About'. Repr. in his *The Importance of What We Care About*. New York: Cambridge University Press, 80–94. First published in 1982.

Garcia, Robert and King, Nathan (eds). 2009. *Is Goodness without God Good Enough?* Lanham, MD: Rowman and Littlefield.

Goetz, Stewart. 2012. *The Purpose of Life: A Theistic Perspective*. London: Continuum.

Gordon, Jeffrey. 1983. 'Is the Existence of God Relevant to the Meaning of Life?' *The Modern Schoolman* 60: 227–46.

Hammerton, Matthew. 2018. 'Well-Being and Meaning in Life'. Presentation given at the First International Conference on Philosophy and Meaning in Life held at Hokkaido University in Sapporo, Japan.

Hartshorne, Charles. 1984. 'God and the Meaning of Life'. In Leroy Rouner (ed.), *On Nature*. Notre Dame: University of Notre Dame Press, 154–68.

Haught, John. 2013. 'Is Nature Enough?' Repr. in Joshua Seachris (ed.), *Exploring the Meaning of Life: An Anthology and Guide*. Malden, MA: Wiley-Blackwell, 173–82. First published in 2006.

Hepburn, R. W. 2000. 'Questions about the Meaning of Life'. Repr. in E. D. Klemke (ed.), *The Meaning of Life*, 2nd edn. New York: Oxford University Press, 261–76. First published in 1966.

Hubin, Donald. 2009. 'Empty and Ultimately Meaningless Gestures?' In Robert Garcia and Nathan King (eds), *Is Goodness without God Good Enough?* Lanham, MD: Rowman and Littlefield, 133–50.

James, Laurence. 2009. 'Shape and the Meaningfulness of Life'. In Lisa Bortolotti (ed.), *Philosophy and Happiness*. New York: Palgrave Macmillan, 54–67.

Kahane, Guy. 2011. 'Should We Want God to Exist?' *Philosophy and Phenomenological Research* 82: 674–96.

Kahane, Guy. 2014. 'Our Cosmic Insignificance'. *Noûs* 48: 745–72.

Kahane, Guy. 2018. 'If There Is a Hole, It Is Not God-Shaped'. In Klaas Kraay (ed.), *Does God Matter? Essays on the Axiological Consequences of Theism*. New York: Routledge, 95–131.

Kekes, John. 2000. 'The Meaning of Life'. In Peter French and Howard Wettstein (eds), *Midwest Studies in Philosophy, Volume 24: Life and Death*. Malden, MA: Blackwell, 17–34.

Kershnar, Stephen. 2014. 'Thad Metz's Fundamentality Theory of Meaning in Life'. *Science, Religion and Culture* 1: 97–100.

Kraay, Klaas. 2018a. 'Invitation to the Axiology of Theism'. In Klaas Kraay (ed.), *Does God Matter? Essays on the Axiological Consequences of Theism*. New York: Routledge, 1–35.

Kraay, Klaas (ed.). 2018b. *Does God Matter? Essays on the Axiological Consequences of Theism*. New York: Routledge.

Kraay, Klaas and Dragos, Chris. 2013. 'On Preferring God's Non-Existence'. *Canadian Journal of Philosophy* 43: 153–78.

Landau, Iddo. 1997. 'Why Has the Question of Life's Meaning Arisen in the Last Two and a Half Centuries?' *Philosophy Today* 41: 263–9.

Lougheed, Kirk. 2017. 'Anti-Theism and the Objective Meaningful Life Argument'. *Dialogue* 56: 337–55.

Lutz, Matthew and Lenman, James. 2018. 'Moral Naturalism' (rev. edn). In Edward Zalta (ed.), *Stanford Encyclopedia of Philosophy*. https://plato .stanford.edu/entries/naturalism-moral/.

Maitzen, Stephen. 2009. 'Ordinary Morality Implies Atheism'. *European Journal for Philosophy of Religion* 2: 107–26.

Maitzen, Stephen. 2018. 'The Problem of Magic'. In Klaas Kraay (ed.), *Does God Matter? Essays on the Axiological Consequences of Theism*. New York: Routledge, 132–46.

Markus, Arjan. 2003. 'Assessing Views of Life'. *Religious Studies* 39: 125–43.

Martela, Frank. 2017. 'Meaningfulness As Contribution'. *Southern Journal of Philosophy* 55: 232–56.

Mawson, T. J. 2013. 'Recent Work on the Meaning of Life and the Philosophy of Religion'. *Philosophy Compass* 8: 1138–46.

Mawson, T. J. 2016. *God and the Meanings of Life: What God Could and Couldn't Do to Make Our Lives More Meaningful*. London: Bloomsbury Publishing.

Mawson, T. J. 2018. 'God's Possible Roles in the Meaning of Life'. *European Journal for the Philosophy of Religion* 10: 193–203.

May, Todd. 2009. *Death*. Stocksfield: Acumen.

Megill, Jason and Linford, Daniel. 2016. 'God, the Meaning of Life, and a New Argument for Atheism'. *International Journal of Philosophy of Religion* 79: 31–47.

Metz, Thaddeus. 2013a. *Meaning in Life*. Oxford: Oxford University Press.

Metz, Thaddeus. 2013b. 'The Meaning of Life' (rev. edn). In Edward Zalta (ed.), *Stanford Encyclopedia of Philosophy*. https://plato.stanford.edu /entries/life-meaning/.

Metz, Thaddeus. 2013c. 'How God Could Assign Us a Purpose without Disrespect'. *Quadranti* 1: 99–112.

Metz, Thaddeus. 2015. 'Assessing Lives, Capturing Naturalism, and Giving Supernaturalism Its Due'. In Masahiro Morioka (ed.), *Reconsidering Meaning in Life*. Saitama, Japan: Waseda University, 228–78.

Metz, Thaddeus. 2016a. 'Further Explorations of Supernaturalism about Meaning in Life'. *European Journal for Philosophy of Religion* 8: 59–83.

Metz, Thaddeus. 2016b. 'Is Life's Meaning Ultimately Unthinkable?' *Philosophia* 44: 1247–56.

Metz, Thaddeus. 2017a. 'Meaning in Life'. In Benjamin Matheson and Yujin Nagasawa (eds), *The Palgrave Handbook on the Afterlife*. New York: Palgrave Macmillan, 353–70.

Metz, Thaddeus. 2017b. 'Neutrality, Partiality, and Meaning in Life'. *De Ethica* 4: 7–25.

Metz, Thaddeus. 2018. 'God's Role in a Meaningful Life'. *European Journal for Philosophy of Religion* 10: 171–91.

Metz, Thaddeus. 2019. 'Meaning'. In Graham Oppy (ed.), *Blackwell Companion to Atheism and Philosophy*. Oxford: Blackwell, 355–66.

Mintoff, Joseph. 2008. 'Transcending Absurdity'. *Ratio* 21: 64–84.

Morris, Thomas. 1992. *Making Sense of It All: Pascal and the Meaning of Life*. Grand Rapids, MI: William B. Eerdmans Publishing Company.

Moser, Paul. 2016. 'Affective Gethsemane Meaning for Life'. In Joshua Seachris and Stewart Goetz (eds), *God and Meaning*. New York: Bloomsbury Academic, 167–84.

Mulgan, Tim. 2015. *Purpose in the Universe: The Moral and Metaphysical Case for Ananthropocentric Purposivism*. Oxford: Oxford University Press.

Nagel, Thomas. 1971. 'The Absurd'. *The Journal of Philosophy* 68: 716–27.

Nagel, Thomas. 1987. *What Does It All Mean?* New York: Oxford University Press.

Norman, Richard. 2006. 'The Varieties of Non-Religious Experience'. *Ratio* 19: 474–94.

Nozick, Robert. 1974. *Anarchy, State and Utopia*. New York: Basic Books.

Nozick, Robert. 1981. *Philosophical Explanations*. Cambridge, MA: Harvard University Press.

Nussbaum, Martha. 1989. 'Mortal Immortals'. *Philosophy and Phenomenological Research* 50: 303–51.

Penner, Myron. 2015. 'Personal Anti-Theism and the Meaningful Life Argument'. *Faith and Philosophy* 32: 325–37.

Penner, Myron. 2017. 'On the Objective Meaningful Life Argument'. *Dialogue* 57: 173–82.

Penner, Myron and Arbour, Benjamin. 2018. 'Arguments from Evil and Evidence for Pro-Theism'. In Klaas Kraay (ed.), *Does God Matter? Essays on the Axiological Consequences of Theism*. New York: Routledge, 192–202.

Poettcker, Jason. 2015. 'Defending the Purpose Theory of Meaning in Life'. In Masahiro Morioka (ed.), *Reconsidering Meaning in Life*. Saitama, Japan: Waseda University, 180–207.

Purves, Duncan and Delon, Nicolas. 2018. 'Meaning in the Lives of Humans and Other Animals'. *Philosophical Studies* 175: 317–38.

Quinn, Philip. 2000. 'How Christianity Secures Life's Meanings'. In Joseph Runzo and Nancy Martin (eds), *The Meaning of Life in the World Religions*. Oxford: Oneworld Publications, 53–68.

Salles, Sagid. 2010. 'O Sentido da Vida e o Propósite de Deus'. *Fundamento* 1: 84–110. English translation is on file with the author.

Sartre, Jean-Paul. 1956. 'Existentialism Is a Humanism'. Walter Kaufmann (trans.). Repr. in Walter Kaufmann (ed.), *Existentialism from Dostoyevsky to Sartre*. New York: The World Publishing Company, 287–311. First published in 1946.

Scarre, Geoffrey. 2007. *Death*. Stocksfield: Acumen.

Scheffler, Samuel. 2013. 'Death and the Afterlife'. In Niko Kolodny (ed.), *Death and the Afterlife*. New York: Oxford University Press, 15–110.

Schellenberg, J. L. 2018. In Klaas Kraay (ed.), *Does God Matter? Essays on the Axiological Consequences of Theism*. New York: Routledge, 181–91.

Seachris, Joshua. 2009. 'The Meaning of Life As Narrative: A New Proposal for Interpreting Philosophy's "Primary" Question'. *Philo* 12: 5–23.

Seachris, Joshua. 2011. 'Death, Futility, and the Proleptic Power of Narrative Ending'. *Religious Studies* 47: 141–63.

Seachris, Joshua. 2013. 'General Introduction'. In Joshua Seachris (ed.), *Exploring the Meaning of Life: An Anthology and Guide*. Malden, MA: Wiley-Blackwell, 1–20.

Seachris, Joshua. 2016. 'The Meaning of Life and Narratives: A Framework for Understanding and Answering the Question of Life's Meaning'. In Joshua Seachris and Stewart Goetz (eds), *God and Meaning*. New York: Bloomsbury Academic, 13–34.

Seachris, Joshua. 2019. 'Meaning of Life: Contemporary Analytic Perspectives'. In James Fieser and Bradley Dowden (eds), *Internet Encyclopedia of Philosophy*. www.iep.utm.edu/mean-ana/.

Singer, Irving. 1996. *Meaning of Life, Volume 1: The Creation of Value*. Baltimore: Johns Hopkins University Press.

Sinnott-Armstrong, Walter. 2009: 'Why Traditional Theism Cannot Provide an Adequate Foundation for Morality'. In Robert Garcia and Nathan King (eds), *Is Goodness without God Good Enough?* Lanham, MD: Rowman and Littlefield, 101–15.

Smith, Huston. 2000. 'The Meaning of Life in the World's Religions'. In Joseph Runzo and Nancy Martin (eds), *The Meaning of Life in the World Religions*. Oxford: Oneworld Publications, 255–68.

Smith, Quentin. 1997. *Ethical and Religious Thought in Analytic Philosophy of Language*. New Haven: Yale University Press.

Smuts, Aaron. 2011. 'Immortality and Significance'. *Philosophy and Literature* 35: 134–49.

Smuts, Aaron. 2013. 'The Good Cause Account of the Meaning of Life'. *Southern Journal of Philosophy* 51: 536–62.

Steinhart, Eric. 2017. 'Digital Afterlives'. In Yujin Nagasawa and Benjamin Matheson (eds), *The Palgrave Handbook of the Afterlife*. London: Palgrave Macmillan, 255–73.

Svenson, David. 2000. 'The Dignity of Human Life'. Repr. in E. D. Klemke (ed.), *The Meaning of Life*, 2nd edn. New York: Oxford University Press, 21–30. First published in 1949.

Swinburne, Richard. 2009. 'What Difference Does God Make to Morality?' In Robert Garcia and Nathan King (eds), *Is Goodness without God Good Enough?* Lanham, MD: Rowman and Littlefield, 151–63.

Swinburne, Richard. 2016. 'How God Makes Life a Lot More Meaningful'. In Joshua Seachris and Stewart Goetz (eds), *God and Meaning*. New York: Bloomsbury Academic, 149–64.

Taliaferro, Charles. 2016. 'The Expansion and Contraction of the Meaning of Life'. In Joshua Seachris and Stewart Goetz (eds), *God and Meaning*. New York: Bloomsbury Academic, 137–47.

Tartaglia, James. 2015. *Philosophy in a Meaningless Life*. London: Bloomsbury.

Taylor, Richard. 1987. 'Time and Life's Meaning'. *The Review of Metaphysics* 40: 675–86.

Taylor, Richard. 2000. *Good and Evil*. Amherst, NY: Prometheus Books. First published in 1970.

Thomson, Garrett. 2003. *On the Meaning of Life*. South Melbourne: Wadsworth.

Tolstoy, Leo. 1884. *A Confession*. Louise Maude and Aylmer Maude (trans.). www.online-literature.com/tolstoy/a-confession/.

Tooley, Michael. 2018. 'Axiology: Theism versus Widely Accepted Monotheisms'. In Klaas Kraay (ed.), *Does God Matter? Essays on the Axiological Consequences of Theism*. New York: Routledge, 46–69.

Trisel, Brooke Alan. 2002. 'Futility and the Meaning of Life Debate'. *Sorites* 14: 70–84.

Trisel, Brooke Alan. 2004. 'Human Extinction and the Value of Our Efforts'. *The Philosophical Forum* 35: 371–91.

Trisel, Brooke Alan. 2012. 'Intended and Unintended Life'. *The Philosophical Forum* 43: 395–403.

Trisel, Brooke Alan. 2016. 'Human Extinction, Narrative Ending, and Meaning of Life'. *Journal of Philosophy of Life* 6: 1–22.

Waghorn, Nicholas. 2014. *Nothingness and the Meaning of Life: Philosophical Approaches to Ultimate Meaning through Nothing and Reflexivity*. London: Bloomsbury.

Waghorn, Nicholas. 2015. 'Metz' Incoherence Objection: Some Epistemological Considerations'. In Masahiro Morioka (ed.), *Reconsidering Meaning in Life*. Saitama, Japan: Waseda University, 150–68.

Walker, Lois Hope. 1989. 'Religion and the Meaning of Life and Death'. In Louis Pojman (ed.), *Philosophy: The Quest for Truth*. Belmont, CA: Wadsworth Publishing Company, 167–71.

Wielenberg, Erik. 2005. *Value and Virtue in a Godless Universe*. Cambridge: Cambridge University Press.

Wielenberg, Erik. 2016. 'Metz's Case against Supernaturalism'. *European Journal for Philosophy of Religion* 8: 27–34.

Wisnewski, J. Jeremy. 2005. 'Is the Immortal Life Worth Living?' *International Journal of Philosophy of Religion* 58: 27–36.

Williams, Bernard. 1973. 'The Makropulos Case: Reflections on the Tedium of Immortality'. In his *Problems of the Self*. Cambridge: Cambridge University Press, 82–100.

Wolf, Susan. 2010. *Meaning in Life and Why It Matters*. Princeton: Princeton University Press.

Wollheim, Richard. 1984. *The Thread of Life*. Cambridge, MA: Harvard University Press.

Cambridge Elements ☰

Philosophy of Religion

CPSIA information can be obtained
at www.ICGtesting.com
Printed in the USA
LVHW081704090820
662559LV00038B/1793

9 781108 457453